Puppet Scripts for Sunday Mornings

Joan M. Sercl

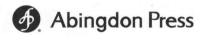

Abingdon Press

Dedicated to the most wonderful caring parents,
Ruth and Henry Lewis, who have guided,
cared, encouraged, and loved me. They have
been very special blessings in my life.

TABLE OF CONTENTS

INTRODUCTION

Hi. I'm glad you picked up this book. It means you are interested in sharing your faith with children through the use of a puppet or puppets. There is something magical about a puppet. A puppet can grasp the attention of even the most distracted of children. Puppets seem to break through our chaotic world and transform lives into an enjoyable experience of laughter, humor and new knowledge.

In a "nutshell" let me share my life. Until I was ten I struggled desperately with extremely crossed eyes. I became very withdrawn, quiet, terribly shy, never spoke up in class. Why would I? All they would see is those horrible crossed eyes. Even after surgery . . . the damage had been done. My parents (Ruth and Henry Lewis) tried to encourage me. My father, a Methodist minister, picked up on my excitement after seeing a puppet show at a Mother-Daughter Banquet. He built me a stage with lights and an automatic curtain. It really was wonderful. Mom made some puppets and scenery. I could go behind the stage and totally let myself go. I gave my social study reports, my book reports . . . all from behind that stage. From here on puppets were in my life. I worked my way through college giving performances. The only period in my life when I did little with puppets was when I had four small daughters (Lindi, Teri, Karen and Sandy) but as they grew we did things together. I did many projects in the church and Sunday School. I directed a Puppet Ministry called the God Squad out of Trinity Lutheran Church in St. Peter, Minnesota. For seven years we traveled five states and shared our message. When I moved to Sioux Falls, S.D. I realized I couldn't afford the time commitment of a puppet ministry, and I had wondered what I could do to share my faith. I had heard of ventriloquism so I went to library and got a few books and started to practice. I ordered a puppet and Esmerelda came in the mail. I did some of the children's sermons at First United Methodist Church in Sioux Falls, SD. When I first started I was only a novice, and it was scary. For the first time I didn't have a stage to hide behind, it was Esmerelda and me right out in front! After quite a few children's messages a woman came up to me and said, "Where do you get your scripts? They are just wonderful!" I thanked her and said I just write my own. "Have you ever thought of publishing them?" Of course I hadn't. But with her urging, I sent them to Abingdon Press. Now you are holding this book in your hand. May God bless you in your work, for sharing God with our young is one of the most vital things you can do. In the following paragraphs I give you some helps in getting started.

THE PUPPET
Personality-Character

So you have a cute puppet, muppet type, or an animal. But who is he or she? What do we know about him? He gives the illusion that he can talk, think, hear, see, and move. Inside of this cloth or wood body, what kind of character is he? That is your job. You must give him a personality. Everything that he says or wears is dependent on his character. He needs to be likeable. If your audience doesn't like your figure they aren't going to relate to him. He can be lovable, sweet, shy, brash, out-spoken, and tough and still be lovable. May I suggest that you sit down and write out the characteristics of this "new person." When Esmerelda arrived these were some of the things I incorporated into her personality:
- She loves riddles *(you will find those sprinkled throughout the scripts)*
- She loves to sing *(I often object because she really isn't very good—works well when you don't sing well)*
- She often speaks before she thinks *(monopolizes the conversations at times)*
- Her favorite expression is "Holy Cow"
- Boys at this point in her life are a point of aggravation
- She will short-cut on work *(her chores and homework)*
- She loves to pick on the preachers *(Congregations love this)*
- Basically she has a kind heart, is honest and feels a sense of fairness
- Questions her faith.

MANIPULATION

I am only going to make one point here—that the manipulation needs to fit your puppet. It it is a perky cute animal, the movements might be quick and light. Grandma or Grandpa would move more slowly; a sophisticated intellectual would have confident movements. A shy, bashful type would shrink away, cover face, look at the floor. Keep movement in character with your puppet. And as your puppet projects his personality be sure that you react to it. Your reactions could be shock, disbelief, surprise, indifference, laughter, embarrassment or yawning in boredom.

Always remember to keep your figure alive. Don't let him die when you are speaking or looking away.

VOICE

The main thing you need to master here is a voice that is different from your natural voice. The voice you will use for your puppet should fit. For example:

    Old man—halting speech, cracked voice
    Old woman—high-pitched, falsetto, creaking
    Shy girl—soft, lispy-higher

6

Uneducated—coarse, ungrammatical

Child of the streets—loud, harsh, ungrammatical

Cultured—rather high voice, very refined, larger vocabulary

In creating your voice, even a few steps higher or lower or speaking faster or slower, can make a difference. Make sure that it doesn't hurt when using your voice. It it's uncomfortable for you, it will also be uncomfortable for those listening.

VENTRILOQUIST OR NOT!

Because I am a ventriloquist does not mean that you must be one to use a puppet. Changing your voice and using a puppet will still add a wonderful dimension to working with children. You will find that they will be watching the puppet and pay very little attention to you, especially if you make that puppet a vibrant personality. Many people would find it hard to commit to the time it takes to keep your lips from moving. If that is the case I would encourage you to share with children in any way that is you.

Another method is pretending to have the puppet whisper in the adult's ear. For example, the adult could hold Daffy Duck up to an ear, then nod and say, "Well, I don't know . . . uh . . . huh . . . I'll ask them. Boys and girls, Daffy Duck wants to know if you like his new hat? What do you think?" The end result is the puppet is acting it out, but always communicating through the adult.

Having a puppet as a class mascot can really be a wonderful tool. If the teacher has a problem or announcements, the class mascot can take over. Example: If sharing is a problem, maybe the teacher could go to the class mascot. "Let's see what Sam thinks about sharing our crayons." Or "Let's all be quiet, Sam has an important announcement to make." I guarantee you will get undivided attention. Somehow a puppet can say the same thing we would and get much better results.

STAGES

If being behind a stage is best for you, here are some ideas for staging. Most are very simple and can he put together with a minimum of effort. See diagrams on pages 191 and 192.

Doorway

Television stage-cardboard box

Apron Stage

Two ladders and a sheet

Church table or cardtable stage

Reversible stage

Cardboard Scene

Rear-view Hand Puppet Stage

Appliance Box

Two chairs and a pole

SCRIPTS

How to use
As you read the scripts keep these points in mind:
- Any word written in CAPS or bold print should be projected or said emphatically.
- All actions are in (parenthesis.)
- . . . indicates pauses

A very important point I want you to remember is that these scripts could be used in many of the following ways:
- Ventriloquist and Puppet (how scripts are written)
- Two puppets carry dialogue (use of stage-optional)
- Older child and a puppet
- Teacher and a child
- Script could be read and told in your own words

Use your imagination!
In these scripts you will see a J which stands for Joan, and an Es which stands for Esmerelda. Most ventriloquist scripts are written with a V for vent and an F for figure. These scripts are written to be shared with you, but I hope you will take as many liberties as seem necessary.
- In many of scripts I have a bit of an introduction using a song or riddles (Esmerelda's favorite). These could be moved around from script to script. You could take the beginning of one script and use it preceding a different script.
- In our church we have quite an age span that comes up for the children's sermons (age 2-age 11) so in writing I have hit the middle ages. If you work with the very young some of the humor may go over their heads and you may want to omit that and use different humor. (See Riddle Section, page 168.) You may select something from this section.
- Use your own experiences. In one script (Sadness, p. 72) I talk about losing a friend. Maybe you could relate a time when you felt very sad. You could use the idea I have suggested, but use your personal experience and it may be more meaningful.
- The very first script in the book introduces a puppet. The first time you use a puppet you should introduce "it" to the children, so they know what she likes and dislikes, her personality, what she likes to do, who's in her family, etc. They develop a relationship with her. Again alter the script to fit your needs.
- Bring in current events, things happening in your city or church or school. In other words personalize as often as you can.
- Esmerelda obviously is female, but if your puppet is a male, just alter the script. In the script Eight Weeks for Delivery you could change the hair clip to a model airplane.
- I always thank the kids for coming up for the sermon. I think it's important that they know their participation is important.

8

MEMORIZATION

Many people feel that memorization is difficult, but really it's fairly easy using a few helpful hints:

    - First go over and over it. Six times will give you a feel of how it moves.

    - Put it on a cassette tape—listen to it over and over until it gets stuck in your mind like a song on the radio. Then while you are listening try to beat the tape to each line as it is played.

    - I like to write KEY WORDS in the margin of the script. From those I make up a sheet of those key words—many times they fit on a recipe card. After I feel I have memorized the script I also have fixed in my mind those key words on the card so as I deliver the dialog I see those key words and it keeps me on track. Note the "Memory Memo" sheet following each script. These give you the script in a "nut-shell," an aid to quicker memorization.

HUMOR

Children love humor! Sometimes the sillier the better. They will laugh at things we think ridiculous. They love rhyme. I've made up silly poems using their names. They love it! As I mentioned earlier some humor in these scripts could be over the heads of young children. In the back you will find a section of additional humor where you could pick and choose what you feel fits your age group. It is categorized as follows: General, Seasonal, Special Days, Weather, Bible, Church, and Sports.

PUPPET RESOURCES

I have included a list of resources that you will find very helpful. See page 10. Many of these have puppets for sale, newsletters, scripts, props, tapes, videos. They have courses on Ventriloquism, really just about anything you'd need to do a better job with puppets. Look them over, send for their catalogs and get started!

Children are by no means a second class audience because of their age. Remember they have watched many hours of T.V. As adults we need to give them the best we can give, leave them with a desire to do better, reach for higher goals, care about others and their families. If we can create a puppet friend that will draw them in and make them excited to know God better . . . Wow! What a wonderful mission! God Bless you!

LIST OF PUPPET RESOURCES

MAHER STUDIOS
P.O. Box 420
Littleton, CO 80160
(303) 798-6830
Fax (303) 798-3160
*(Puppets, Ventriloquism
supplies, scripts, videos,
catalog, newsletter)*

MAI Puppets
708 Red Lane
Salem, VA 24153
(703) 389-2528
(Puppets and catalog)

ONE WAY STREET
Box 2398
Littleton, CO 80161
(303) 790-1188
*(Catalog, tapes, videos,
lighting, newsletter, scripts,
puppets, etc.)*

PUPPET PALS
Dept. H
6686 Lee Street
Arvada, CO 80004
*(Catalog, tapes, scripts,
puppets)*

KINGDOM KARACTERS
108 S. Shore Drive
Elkton, MD 21921
(410) 885-5050
*(Brochure, newsletter
annually, puppets, stages,
workshops)*

PUPPET PRODUCTIONS
P.O. Box 1066
DeSoto, TX 75123
(800) 854-2151
*(Catalog, tapes, videos,
scripts, puppets)*

CARAWAY STREET INC.
11605 44th Place North
Plymouth, MN 55442
(800) 767-0678
*(Brochure on Caraway St.
Program, promotional video)*

BIBLE TRUE AUDIO
VISUALS
1441 South Busse Road
Mount Prospect, IL 60056
*(Catalog, tapes, videos,
scripts, puppets)*

SON SHINE PUPPET
COMPANY
P.O. Box 6203
Rockford, IL 61125
(800) 257-8773
*(Catalog, newsletter, tapes,
videos, books, walk-around
costumes, Spanish and
English childrens' ministry
materials)*

THE PUPPET PLACE
3475 Market Street
Camp Hill, PA 17011
(717) 761-4694
(Catalog, newsletter, puppets)

PRINCE PUPPETS
4819 King Road
Allison Park, PA 15101
(412) 443-0932
*(Catalog, newsletter, tapes,
puppets)*

OTHER RESOURCES

THE PUPPETRY STORE
1525 24th S.E.
Auburn, WA 98002
*(Puppet related books, scripts,
patterns,
audio and video tapes)*

ORGANIZATIONS

PUPPETEERS OF
AMERICA
#5 Cricklewood Path
Pasadena, CA 91107-1002
*(Check your yellow pages for
one in your region)*
*(Newsletter—local and
national)*

FELLOWSHIP OF
CHRISTIAN PUPPETEERS
Mail Center-Box 423
Windham, ME 04062
(Directory-national)

DIALOGUE MAGAZINE
Att: Bob Ladd
103 Ironwood Court
Vinton, VA 24179
(540) 890-3397
*(Voice of the Ventroloquist-
Quarterly-send $2 for sample
copy)*

NORTH AMERICAN
ASSOCIATION OF
VENTROLOQUISTS-
N.A.A.V.
P.O. Box 420
Littleton, CO 80160
*(Members receive
announcements of new
products, special events,
shows and workshops-Maher
Messenger newsletter)*

INTRODUCTION OF PUPPET

J   Good Morning, kids. This is the day I told you we would have a very special guest.

Es   Is that me?

J   Boys and girls, this is Esmerelda. *(or name of your puppet)*

Es   *(Looks around)* Hey, where are we?

J   This is _____ Church. *(name of church)* Remember I told you?

Es   Holy Cow, this is really cool! *(Looks around—could comment on any outstanding features of sanctuary)* That cross is sure neat.

J   Esmerelda, we are really excited that you decided to come to our church.

Es   I didn't come . . . I was mailed.

J   Really? Where were you born?

Es   I wasn't born. I was sewn.

J   I guess you are right. I found you in a catalog ...I sent for you.

Es   How many box tops did you need?

J   Esmerelda, no box tops, just cold cash!

Es   How much?

J   Well, let's see . . . about $30.

Es   Holy Cow, that's lot of money for a hunk of cloth.

J   You are a very interesting piece of cloth. In fact I really like your dress. *(could comment on color, style, etc. or any outstanding feature of the puppet)*

Es   Yep, K-Mart blue light special.

J   *(Joannie frowns a bit, looking down at puppet's feet, then says slowly)* Esmerelda, you have your shoes on the wrong feet.

Es   *(Esmerelda looks at one foot, then the other a few times)* How could I, these are the only feet I have!

11

J   And that is a very interesting pair of socks. One is red and one is blue.

Es   *(looks again)* Yep, and I have another pair just like them at home!

J   I can see this is going to be a very interesting friendship . . . Esmerelda, seeing as this is your first Sunday here, how about if I interview you so that we all can get to know you better?

Es   Okey, Dokie!

J   Let's see . . . first off, what is your favorite thing to eat?

Es   Junk food!

J   Junk food, and just what is your definition of Junk Food?

Es   Junk food is what they call anything that tastes good.

J   *(Slowly)* O . . . K . . . let's see, do you have a favorite sport?

Es   Oh yes, I absolutely love Baseball. My friend Alice says, I'm a fanatic . . . she says all I ever read is about baseball . . . all I ever talk about is baseball . . . all I ever think about is baseball.

J   Really?

Es   I told her she's way off base!

J   How about school, do you like school?

Es   Sure.

J   Do you mind if I check you out and see how you are doing?

Es   I guess so . . .

J   Let's start with some words. What is the opposite of JOY?

Es   Sorrow

J   The opposite of Misery?

Es   Happiness

J   That's right. Now the opposite of Woe?

Es   Giddap

J   *(disgusted look)* Let's try a little math. If I have 10 apples and I ate nine of them, what will I have?

12

Es A bellyache!

J No, I mean how many apples will I have left?

Es Oh, you mean if I had ten apples and you ate nine, how many would I have left?

J Yes.

Es None!

J What?

Es I ate the other apple!

J What else do you like to do, Es?

Es I absolutely . . . . love to sing.

J That's wonderful. We do lots of singing here and we sure could use a good voice. Can you sing something for us?

Es *(In a rather awful voice—to the tune of Clementine)* Oh my Darlin', Oh my Darlin', Oh my Darlin Calvin Klein . . .

J Es, for Pete's Sakes, it's not Calvin Klein, it's Clementine.

Es It is?

J Well, I guess you modernized that one. *(clears throat)* Ummmm, let's move on here. What else do you like?

Es I really, really like riddles.

J Oh, no!

Es What's the matter?

J Riddles! I hate riddles. I can NEVER figure them out.

Es Good. Here's one for you. *(Joannie look of "oh no")* Who was the most popular actor in the Bible?
J Haven't the slightest . . .

Es . . . Sampson

J Sampson?

13

Es Yey, he brought the house down. Got another one. Who was the straightest man in the Bible?

J The straightest man? Es . . . !

Es It was Joseph. Pharaoh made a ruler out of him!

J Now that you have totally SHOWN me up . . .

Es I wouldn't do that for all the Barbie dolls in Toys R Us.

J You haven't got me convinced. Say, did you go to Sunday School this morning?

Es I sure did!

J What did they talk about?

Es Well, we talked about Joshua fightin' the BATTLE OF GERITOL.

J ESMERELDA! I see you are certainly going to keep us on our toes here at _____ *(name of church)* We need to bring this to a close.

Es I have one more riddle . . .

J Oh no, no more riddles . . .

Es What did one penny say to another penny?

J C'mon Es, this is really embarrassing!

Es *(slowly)* Together we make sense.

J Cute . . . Well, Esmerelda, we're sure gonna try!

14

NEW YEARS "REVOLUTIONS"

<u>IDEA:</u> *New Year's Resolutions, excuses and a new year is God's gift*
<u>PROP:</u> *List of New Year's Resolutions*

Es *(Sings)* Should Auld Acquaintances be forgot and never brought to mind
. . . *(continues few lines)*

J Esmerelda, what are you doing?

Es Well, I'm still celebrating the New Year.

J Listen, you can't just celebrate, you've got to get on with it, make plans,
get organized. This is a brand new year!

Es Yep, I'm way ahead of you. I have a whole list of "revolutions" here.
(brings forth a long list)

J Es, it's RESOLUTIONS, not REVOLUTION. Let me see that . . *(begins
reading . . .)* make my bed every day, help with the dishes without being
asked, quit arguing with my little sister, do better . . *(turns to Esmerelda)*
Listen, Esmerelda, this is the same list as last year.

Es I know, I decided I better run it through again, seeing as I didn't do so
great last year.

J Why is that . . why didn't you do these things?

Es Well, it's this way. In the winter you put two blankets on my bed and that
makes it really hard to make. By the time I finish watching my favorite
TV show you're always done with the dishes and . . . as for my little sister,
she's impossible to get along with sometimes.

J Es, you know what?

Es What?

J I think you should call these New Year's Excuses instead of Resolutions.

Es Excuses!

J Yes, excuses. Those are the reasons you find not to do what you planned
. . . and you know what else?

Es What?

J Revolutions really isn't such a bad word for your New Year's Resolutions
because when something revolves, it comes around again, and because

15

you didn't do anything about last year's resolutions you have to make them over again.

Es   Is this a lecture on responsibility?

J   Not really, Esmerelda, but you can't build a reputation on what you are GOING to do. You need to DO it!

Es   Well, there is one good thing about putting things off . . .

J   There is?

Es   Yep, you always have something to do tomorrow!

J   Esmerelda!

Es   I may not be good at New Year's Resolutions, but I'm charming, interesting and irresistible!

J   *(shocked look)* I'll tell you something else . . . Praise can be great . . . as long as you don't aim it at yourself!

Es   Guess I'm not doing too well, am I?

J   Es, do you like gifts?

Es   Well of course, who wouldn't?

J   Well, look at it this way . . . this year is God's gift to you.

Es   A year . . . a gift?

J   Yes, Es, and use this year to show God how you love him.

Es   I know God is happy when I'm kind, when I show love to others . . . when I care.

J   You've got it!

Es   I'll say the prayer today:
Dear God
Thank you for a new year. Help me to live each day for you, God. This year is your gift to me . . . thank you.
Amen.

J   HAPPY NEW YEAR to each of you.

Memory Memo
(NEW YEAR'S REVOLUTIONS)

SINGS—AULD ACQUAINTANCES
- Brand new year
- List—resolutions
  - make bed
  - help dishes
  - quit arguing
- Same list last year

NEW YEAR'S EXCUSES

"REVOLUTIONS"—Come around again
- Always something to do tomorrow
- Es—charming, interesting, irresistible

PRAISE—Aim at self
YEAR—God's gift—Use it well

PRAYER — HAPPY NEW YEAR

ONLY ONE SAID THANK-YOU
(Taken from Ten Lepers—Luke 17:11-19)

<u>IDEA:</u> *Being thankful*

J   Hi kids.

Es   Hey kids, I have a riddle.

J   C'mon Es, really . . . You and your riddles . . .

Es   Where do cow artists put their works of art?

J   Where do cow artists put their works of art? Spare me the suspense!

Es   In a moooooooseum.

J   Is that right?

Es   All right, what do you get if you cross a bear with a skunk?

J   A bear with a skunk? Once again, I haven't the slightest idea.

Es   Winnie the Phew!

J   Okay, okay, that's great plenty. Now I have a question for you and the kids.

Es   Shoot!

J   Have any of you ever forgotten to say thank-you?

Es   That's sure a strange question. Haven't you got a more interesting question? Like . . .

17

J Es, I'm asking the question!

Es *(hangs head)* Okay.

J Anyone? *(Let children respond here before Esmerelda speaks)*

Es One time Mrs. Jones gave me some cookies . . . and they looked so good I put them in my mouth, so of course I couldn't say a word. *(muffled voice—end of sentence)*

J I'm sure that's true . . . I've seen you eat cookies.

Es Then once my teacher stayed after school to try and help me with my math . . . I guess I should've said thank-you cuz I could tell she was in a hurry to leave that night.

J Well, kids and Esmerelda, in the Bible is the story about Ten Lepers. You see in Bible times there was a very serious disease and they called it leprosy. People who had that disease had to stay outside the city. They couldn't go home to their families. Anytime someone came close to them, they had to shout, "Unclean, unclean" so no one would come near them.

Es How awful! You mean they couldn't even go home to sleep in their bed, or play with the dog?

J No Es, they couldn't. And if a child got it, the mother couldn't hug him or read stories. They couldn't go to school . . . they were all alone.

Es I don't think I like this story.

J Well, one day Jesus came and he saw the Ten Lepers and they cried out, "Jesus, Master, have mercy on us."

Es Did he?

J Oh yes, Esmerelda. He healed them and Jesus said, "Go show yourself to the priest." *(to children)* You see, before they could go home they had to go to the priest and prove they were well again.

Es Wow! *(with enthusiasm)* I'll bet they were excited! *(With great enthusiasm)*

J Esmerelda, they must've been happier than all Christmases and all Birthdays rolled into one. Kids, how many of those ten lepers do you think said thank-you? *(Listen for responses, four, five, etc.—then turn to Esmerelda)* What do you think, Es?

Es Holy Cow! I bet they all said thank-you for something like that!

J Esmerelda . . . only one said "Thank-you."

18

Es ONLY ONE!

J Yes.

Es But there were ten who had that Leprosy stuff.

J You're right.

Es That's disgusting! Jesus must've been really sad.

J When that one person came back and thanked him, Jesus said, "Were not ten made clean?"

Es I would've said "thank you."

J But Es, you forgot to thank Mr. Jones for the cookies, and your teacher . . . remember? We all forget sometimes, but we need to try and remember.

Es Boy, it sure is important!

J Think about this . . . when you got ready to come to Sunday School today, who bought your clothes that you have on? Who bought these shoes? Who put gas in the car so you could get here?

Es Oh. . . oh . . . it isn't too late, is it, Joannie?

J It's never too late to thank someone, Es.

Es And Joannie . . . *(looks at Joannie)* . . . I'll bet you'd really be thankful if I said the prayer today.

J Thanks, Esmerelda! Shall we pray.

Es God, thank you for Jesus who cared so much for each of us. Help me and all my friends here to remember to say thank-you when people do nice things for us. And special thanks to you, God, for this wonderful world you have made for us. Amen.

(or if near Thanksgiving)

Dear God,
Thanksgiving is coming. It's a good time to remember to thank all those who help us. And a special thanks to you, God, for all the good stuff you do for us. Amen.

J And I want to thank all you kids for coming here today, and thanks, Esmerelda, for helping me out.

Es *(louder and fading off as you leave)* Thank-you, thank-you, thank-you . . . thank-you.

19

MEMORY MEMO
(ONLY ONE SAID "THANK-YOU")

RIDDLES
- cows—art work
- cross bear/skunk

QUESTION—forgot—say thank-you
- children response
- Esmerelda
  - Mrs. Jones
  - Teacher

TEN LEPERS
- serious disease—leprosy
- "Unclean"
- couldn't—home, sleep bed, play dog

- Jesus healed—priest
- Happier than Christmas-Birthday
- only one said "Thank-you"
- Remember—who bought clothes, shoes, Sunday school

NEVER TOO LATE TO SAY THANK-YOU

PRAYER

LOVE IS THE BEST GIFT
(Matthew 2:1-12)

<u>IDEA:</u> *Wise man's gifts and what is the best gift?*
<u>PROP:</u> *Esmerelda is wearing slippers instead of shoes.*

J   Esmerelda, I need you to help me today.

Es   OK.

J   We're going to talk about the Wise Men, and I'd like all the children to come forward.

Es   I'll start *(begins singing We Three Kings)* We Three Kings of Orient . . . This is the prelude . . . *(begins singing again)* We Three . . .

J   Es, we don't need a prelude . . . wait until everyone gets down here. *(few seconds)*

Es   Can I start?

J   Not yet.

Es   Now?

J   Esmerelda, just be patient, please! *(all children seated)*

J   Okay, I'm going to ask you all a question . . . how many of you got presents for Christmas?

Es   I did! I got new slippers . . . oh, oh . . .

20

J   What's the matter?

Es   I forgot my shoes.

J   *(in awe, looks at Esmerelda's feet)* Esmerelda, you didn't!

Es   Oh well, now they can see my new slippers.

J   *(hold up Esmerelda's foot)* Now that we know Esmerelda got new slippers
. . . what did some of the rest of you get for Christmas?
(Listen to children's response)

J   Do you know why we give gifts at Christmas? *(If no answers)* Can anyone
guess? *(If no correct answers—proceed)*

Es   I know.

J   You do?

Es   Yep, you told me if no one answered I was 'spose to tell.

J   Okay, let's hear it!

Es   Well, when the Wise Men came searching for Jesus, they brought Gold,
Frankinscense and Myrrh as gifts. So now we give gifts to each other.

J   Good, Esmerelda, you remembered.

Es   I always remember.

J   Not always.

Es   *(emphatic)* Oh yes, I do!

J   *(rather disgusted)* We're not arguing here!

Es   I'm confused . . . it's Jesus' birthday, but we give gifts to others. I'd feel
awful if it was my birthday and everyone gave to someone else.

J   Es, the very nicest gift you could give to Jesus is being kind and loving to
others.

Es   Yeh.

J   You could start with your own family, like your mom.

Es   I gave her a real neat necklace. It said, "#1 Mom."

J   That's really nice, but I don't mean things . . . how could you show you
really love her?

Es I got it! I could keep my clothes neat . . . help with the dishes . . take my boots off at the door . . . when I track on the floor she gets really, really mad!

J Those are great ideas! How about your dad. How could you show your love for him?

Es I guess I could be more appreciative.

J Like how?

Es Well, he always says there are so many bills . . . electric bill, gas bill, grocery bills. I could say "thanks" and turn the lights off more often.

J Esmerelda, that's good. And what about your brother and sister?

Es Ohhhhhhhhh . . . that's very hard. They are impossible sometimes.

J You are never impossible, are you?

Es Never . . . well maybe . . . it's so hard . . .

J Why?

Es Well, brothers and sisters, they mess your room, take your stuff . . . I just get so angry.

J Things could be different, Esmerelda, by being patient and kind.

Es I know . . . I know . . . *(slowly as if trying to understand)* . . .
the gift of love is the very best gift.

J You got it!

Es I guess you could get all the neat things in the world that you wanted, but if no one loved you . . . well, it just wouldn't mean much.

J "LOVE IS THE BEST GIFT OF ALL!" And Baby Jesus was God's gift of Love to us.

Es Wow! Love really is the best gift of all. I learned a song about it in Sunday School.

J How does it go?

Es *(Sings)* Love is something if you give it away, give it away, give it away. Love is something if you give it away . . .
You end up having more.

J How true. Thanks boys and girls and Happy New Year.

22

Es Happy New Year.

J Shall we pray: O God, thank you for your gift of love. Help us to show our love to our friends and family this week.   Amen.

MEMORY MEMO
(LOVE IS THE BEST GIFT)

SINGS: WE THREE KINGS

QUESTION: Got for Christmas?
- Slippers
WHY GIVE CHRISTMAS GIFTS?
- Gold, Frankenscense, Myrrh
- Nicest gift—Being kind
MOTHER
- clothes neat
- dishes
- boots off

FATHER
-Bills (gas, electric, grocery)
BROTHERS_SISTERS
- Mess room
- take stuff
- get angry

LOVE IS THE BEST GIFT OF ALL
SONG:
Love is Something if you Give it Away

FINISH THE TASK

<u>IDEA:</u> *New Year's Resolutions and finishing the task begun.*
<u>PROPS:</u> *List of Resolutions*

J Hi Kids! Hi Esmerelda (or name of puppet, child, etc.)

Es Hello.

J Here we are _____ *(number) week(s)* into the New Year.

Es Already? Yeh I know, I had such a great Christmas. I was just thinking that basketball goes into overtime, football goes into overtime, _____ *(name of pastor)* goes into overtime. When you give me an attitude lecture you sure go into overtime . . . I sure wish Christmas went into overtime.

J Esmerelda, it is really a great season, but we just need to carry the special message of love into the new year.

Es Sure is hard sometimes.

J Your homework is much improved. How do you account for that?

Es I quit asking you for help!

J *(shock)* Esmerelda! Do you have your homework done for Monday?

23

Es I'll finish it tomorrow.

J Es, "never put off to tomorrow what you can do today."

Es Oh great! Let's finish off those donuts we had for breakfast!

J Esmerelda, I am really serious.

Es One thing I'd like to put off is getting up so early to do my paper route. It's cold . . . and miserable!

J The trouble with you is that you are a bit lazy. Why, when I was your age, I thought nothing of getting up at 5 o'clock in the morning.

Es Well, I don't think much of it either.

J Esmerelda, where were you yesterday afternoon?

Es I was helping our neighbor, Mr. Nelson, get the snow off his roof.

J How did it go?

Es Okay, I guess. I knocked over the ladder once though.

J Did you tell Mr. Nelson?

Es He knew . . . he was on the ladder!

J OH NO! *(hand over mouth)* ESMERELDA!

Es I made some New Year's Resolutions.

J Some what?

Es Some New Year's Resolutions . . . you know those promises you make to yourself and keep for a week.

J Do you have them?

Es Yeah, right here. *(holds up arm—paper with resolutions tucked in the sleeve of the puppet)*

J Can I read them?

Es Sure.

J *(takes paper out of puppet's cuff and reads:)*
1. Get my homework done on time

2. Don't complain about my paper route
3. Help my neighbors

Es See what I mean. I messed up on all of them.

J Es, you know we all do, and these are good *(holds out paper to examine again)*. God is pleased when we do our best and finish what we begin, even if it doesn't turn out as planned.

Es Well, it sure didn't!

J Do you see that thermometer over there. *(points to Building Fund Thermometer or use goal in your church)*

Es Yeah.

J When that thermometer is all red this church will have raised the money needed for our new plans and dreams we have here.

Es Wow! It's almost there.

J But we're trying to finish the task and it's been hard work, and the last little bit seems to be the hardest.

Es Yeah, I know some people give God credit, but hesitate to give Him cash.

J You are right there . . . we need everyone's help. Some are so very generous. We all want this dream to come true.

Es Did you know someone gave me a dollar for New Years?

J Well, how nice. What are you going to do with it?

Es Take it to Sunday School.

J I guess you want to show it to your teacher.

Es Nah, I'm going to give it to God. I think he will be as surprised as I was to get something besides nickels.

J That is just great, Esmerelda!
Shall we pray:
Dear God
Help us to finish the tasks we begin. Whether it's cleaning our room, picking up toys or trying to be kind. Help us to never give up, because we know you are our God, and our friend.
Amen.

MEMORY MEMO
(FINISH THE TASK)

OVERTIME
- Basketball
- Football
- Pastor
- You

HOMEWORK
-Quit—you for help
-Finished?
-Donuts

PAPER ROUTE
- Early
- Lazy

NEW YEAR'S RESOLUTION
- Homework done on time
- Not complain—paper route
- help neighbors
- Messed up

FINISH WHAT WE BEGIN
-Thermometer
-New plans and dreams
-Give God credit—no cash

DOLLAR

PRAYER

B IN ATTITUDE

<u>IDEA:</u> *Beatitudes, Matthew 5:1-12*

Es Hey, Joannie. You know my friend Lou? He got a puppy for Christmas. I told him I asked for a puppy, but you said I couldn't have one.

J *(Emphatic!)* Esmerelda, I told you we just couldn't have a dog.

Es Well, Lou told me I didn't ask right.

J You didn't ask right?

Es Yep, he said I should ask for a baby brother . . . then you'll get the dog!

J Oh, really!

Es Hey, I got one for you, Joannie . . . Why did the girl eat bullets.

J Please, Es . . . tell us.

Es She wanted to grow bangs . . .

J *(Look of "oh really")*

Es Okay . . . who killed Capt. Crunch?

J Esmerelda . . . *(irritated)* I don't know who killed Capt. Crunch. Who did?

Es I don't know, but they suspect a CEREAL killer!

J You certainly have a way of getting us off track. In the scripture lesson this morning in Matt. 5:1-12 we are reading about the Sermon on the Mount where Jesus gave us the Beatitudes.

Es   I got one of those in school.

J   Got what?

Es   I got a B in Attitude.

J   You got a B in Attitude . . . *(thinks)* . . . Oh, I see . . . I'm going to act like a mother here . . . *(looks at puppet)* why didn't you get an A in Attitude?

Es   My teacher says I talk too much.

J   You know, Esmerelda, sometimes you can learn a lot more by listening, instead of always talking.

Es   If someone is gonna' listen, then someone has to talk. I figured it might as well be me . . . *(continues to babble)* . . . and you know . . .

J   Will you listen a minute?

Es   *(reluctantly)* Okay.

J   When Jesus gave the sermon on the Mount, and he gave people the Beatitudes, He gave them hope.

Es   What were they hoping for?

J   Well, Es, they were discouraged . . . some were poor or hungry. And Jesus made them feel that even tho they felt that way . . . if they believed . . . life would be better.

Es   How did He do that?

J   You see Esmerelda, in Bible times, there were many laws, but often Jesus would turn the law around.

Es   He did?

J   For example: Jesus said, "the law says an eye for an eye and a tooth for a tooth, *(could explain here)* but I say unto you, Love your enemies."

Es   It's hard, Joannie, that time Todd threw a rock at me . . . well I just threw one back, got him too! *(thinking)* But I guess Jesus' way is kinder.

J   Exactly, Es. Some of the beatitudes are hard to understand, but some you can . *(use a paper or Bible here with beatitudes)* . . . Like here . . . *(points)* "Blessed are they that mourn, for they shall be comforted."

Es   That means if you are sad, you'll feel better?

J   Yes, another:
"Blessed are they that hunger and thirst, they shall be filled."

Es   That means if you're hungry you'll get a sandwich and a coke.

J   Well, sorta. But it isn't always food. Sometimes we are hungry to learn, to make our lives better. *(points)* Here's one, "Blessed are the merciful, for they shall obtain mercy". It means being kind, Es.

Es   I get it . . . if you are kind, kindness will come back to you.

J   Exactly.

Es   Jesus made people want to do better, didn't he?

J   He sure did! Es, what makes us want to do better . . . to be better people?

Es   Attitude?

J   Attitude has a lot to do with it. Attitude is our way of thinking. Jesus had a way of making us want to change.

Es   Guess I could change MY thinking. Instead of a B in ATTITUDE, I'll try for an A in ATTITUDE.

J   Es, if you can quit talking, I think you've hit the nail on the head!
Shall we pray:
Dear God: In the sermon on the Mount, Jesus gave people hope. We too can give hope. Help us, Lord, to LISTEN to what the Beatitudes say to us. Amen.

MEMORY MEMO
(B IN ATTITUDE)

IDEA: Beatitudes
PROP: Bible

PUPPY: Ask baby brother
EAT BULLETS: Grow bangs!
WHO KILLED CAPT. CRUNCH?—
Cereal Killer

BEATITUDES: MATT: 5:1-12
    - Got B in attitude—A in attitude
    - Talk too much
    - learn—listening

JESUS GAVE HOPE
    - Poor—Hungry—believe
    - Laws—Jesus turned around
    - Eye for eye—threw rock

- Beatitudes
    -Blessed mourn—"sad-feel better"
    -Blessed hunger/thirst—
        "sandwich/coke"*(not always food)*
    -Blessed merciful—"kind/kindness
        comes back"

JESUS WANTED PEOPLE TO DO BETTER
- WHAT MAKES US WANT TO DO BETTER—ATTITUDE
- INSTEAD OF B IN ATTITUDE—A IN ATTITUDE
PRAYER

A TREE WITH A VIEW

IDEA: *Story of Zacchaeus (Luke 19:1-10)*
PROP: *Biblical headdress*

J   Good morning, kids. Don't they look great, Esmerelda?

Es   *(half-heartedly)* Yeah.

J   Where's your enthusiasm this morning?

Es   You know, Joannie, there should be a law against having school when there's enough snow to play in.

J   That WAS a beautiful snow this week.

Es   Of course we shouldn't have school in the fall either when there's leaves to play in, or spring when it starts to get nice and warm . . . well, maybe I could go to school a couple days in November and a few in March.

J   Honestly, Esmerelda, by second grade you'd be packing a cane with your lunch.

Es   And by third grade I could retire!

J   Listen, it really can't be all that bad. You told me you had a really good program this week in school on fire safety.

Es   Yeah, it was real cool once I could see.

J   What do you mean?

Es   Well, the First Grade kids sat in front of us, and they have a very tall teacher! Guess where she sat? . . . Right in front of me . . . all I could see was her shoulders . . . nothing else . . . nothing else at all.

J   So what did you do?

Es   Well, first I tried sitting on my back-pack . . .

J   Yeah?

Es   I forgot my lunch was in there . . . my banana looked like it went through the wringer . . . so then I climbed up a ladder they had against the wall in the gym . . . that was perfect until my teacher told me to come down.

J   You remind me of a man in the Bible who did the same thing.

Es Smashed his banana?

J No, no, he climbed a tree so he could see better . . . his name was Zacchaeus.

Es Zach-who-is?

J C'mon, Esmerelda . . . I know you've heard of Zacchaeus, remember . . . *(sings)* "Zacchaeus was a wee little man and a wee little man was he . . ."

Es Spare us, Joannie!

J Esmerelda, I have an idea . . . let's pretend that you are Zacchaeus and I'll interview you. *(Option: could put Biblical headdress on puppet here)*

Es I'm pretty important, huh?

J Well . . .

Es Like really important . . .

J Es, let's just get on with it. Can you tell us where you were born?

Es Sewn.

J Run that by me again.

Es Sewn.

J What on earth is that 'spose to mean'?

Es Puppets are 'sewn' not born.

J Okay, okay, tell me about your childhood.

Es It'll be SHORT.

J What?

Es I had a real SHORT-AGE of height.

J What was it like when you were in school?

Es Well, I always took a SHORT-CUT to school, my friends were in SHORT-SUPPLY.

J Why was that?

Es Maybe because I hated being SHORT and I became very SHORT-TEMPERED about all the "short-people" jokes.

J   Did you have any favorite food or sports you like?

Es   Not really . . . well I love Strawberry SHORT-CAKE and I always played SHORT-STOP on the baseball team.

J   Goodness, all this "short stuff" is getting rather much.

Es   Knock it off, Joannie, not you too!

J   So what happened?

Es   Well, I wasn't very good at baseball so that was SHORT-LIVED, and I became a Tax Collector.

J   Was it a good profession?

Es   Yeah, I SHORT-CHANGED many people, so I made lots of money. In SHORT I was a rich man.

J   So you must've been happy . . . to be so rich.

Es   No . . . I was miserable . . . no one liked me . . . I didn't have any friends.

J   Sounds like something had to change.

Es   Yeah . . . and it did. One day this man Jesus came to town, the crowds were all around him . . . once again being so SHORT I decided the only way I was going to see this wonderful man was to climb up a tree. I found a Sycamore tree . . . and climbed up into the branches.

J   Wow!

Es   When Jesus got to the tree he looked up and said, "Zacchaeus, I'm coming to your house today."

J   Boy, you must've been excited!

Es   I was so excited I got my robe caught in the tree.

J   What an honor to have Jesus come to your house.

Es   The people in my town were horrified that Jesus would come to my house, as I was called a "sinner."

J   Jesus loves even the sinner.

Es   He said that, Joannie. He said God loved tall people, short ones, fat, skinny, well . . . just everyone, and he really cared about me.

J   I guess the real Zacchaeus just didn't realize that.

31

Es Among other things I was SHORT-SIGHTED. So I told Jesus that anyone I had cheated I would pay back four times.

J Zacchaeus was a new man after Jesus touched his life.

Es I'm so glad that everyone over-looked my SHORT-COMINGS and forgave me . . . you know when Jesus is your friend you want to be different.

J Great interview, Esmerelda . . . er . . . Zacchaeus. Guess we could've SHORTENED it up, but then you couldn't have gotten all that SHORT-STUFF in there. Shall we pray:
God,
We thank you for your son, Jesus, who made life so good, by forgiving and loving and caring. May we remember to do the same this week. Amen.

MEMORY MEMO
(A TREE WITH A VIEW)

ENTHUSIASM?
SHOULDN'T HAVE SCHOOL
- snow
- fall—leaves
- spring—nice
- 2nd grade—cane
- 3rd grade—retire

FIRE-SAFETY PROGRAM
- Couldn't see
- Back-pack—lunch
  —banana

ZACCHAEUS
- Sing
- "Spare us"

INTERVIEW
- Born—sewn
-Childhood
-SHORT- SHORT-CUT—school
-SHORT-SUPPLY—friends
- Food: STRAWBERRY SHORT-CAKE
- Sport: SHORT-STOP—SHORT-LIVED
- SHORT-CHANGED—people

JESUS CAME TO TOWN
- Climbed Sycamore tree
- Come to house
- Sinner
- SHORT-SIGHTED—pay back four times
- SHORT-COMINGS—overlooked
Could've SHORTENED it up!

INFECTION VS. AFFECTION
VALENTINE SCRIPT

<u>IDEA:</u> *Love, being an encourager*
<u>PROPS:</u> *Valentine secured in hand of puppet*

Es *(sings)* Happy Birthday to you . . .

J Es, this is not a birthday.

Es We wish you a Merry Christmas . . . we wish you . . . *(sings)*

J Es, for Pete's Sakes . . . it's February.

Es Oh yeah . . . *(sings again)* Christ the Lord is risen today . . .

32

J And it's not Easter either . . . this is Valentine's Day.

Es Oh great . . . I've been waiting for that to happen. I have a good song for that too.

J *(rather disgusted)* Oh great!

Es *(sings)* Let me call you Sweetheart, I'm in love with you, let me hear you whisper that you love me too . . .

J Esmerelda, before you get into all that mushy stuff, I think we should move on here. It sure is hard to imagine that it is Valentine's Day already.

Es Yeah, and I bought you a box of candy . . . chocolate covered cherries.

J Really. Well that is really nice.

Es I thought so too, seeing as I would've much rather had chocolate covered nuts! If I'd had a little more money I'd gotten you one of those boxes with the road map in them.

J What? A road map?

Es You know the chart that tells you where all the good ones are located. Now you can get "eye strain" and "tooth decay at the same time!

J Valentine's Day really is a nice holiday, don't you think, Es? It gives us a chance to say how we feel about someone.

Es Joannie, can I ask you something?

J Sure.

Es What is an "in . . . in . . . fec . . . tion?"

J Well, an infection is when you get a disease or get sick.

Es Oh dear me! I certainly better stay away from that Ryan then.

J Really? How's that?

Es He forgot his lunch at school today, so I shared mine with him.

J That was very nice of you.

Es Yes, I thought so too especially since that was the best sandwich you made all week.

J Yeah . . .

Es Well, when we were leaving he looked at me kinda' funny and said he had a great "infection" for me.

33

J *(laughing)* For Pete's sake, Esmerelda, I think what Ryan meant to say was he had a great "affection" for you.

Es Then what does af . . . fec . . . tion mean, Joannie?

J Well, Es, it means . . . like love.

Es Love! Yuck!

J What's wrong with that?

Es Kissin' and huggin' and all that ol' mushy stuff? Yuck!

J No, no Esmerelda. You've got it all wrong. There's much more to love than that.

Es There is? What do you mean?

J Just being nice and caring about one another is love.

Es Really? You mean you can love someone without all that kissin' and huggin'?

J Of course! One example I can give you of love is being an encourager. *(Es looks confused)* It means helping those around you do their best.

Es Really?

J Remember when I was trying to learn how to be a ventriloquist . . . do you remember what you said?

Es You mean when I said there were lots of Vents who were a lot worse than you?

J I tried to take it as a compliment. *(bit dejected)* But remember when you told your friend Lou, she did race great at the track meet.

Es Yeah . . . that was really hard, 'cuz I wanted to win.

J I also remember when you told Martin he was a math whiz, and told Lisa she had pretty hair.

Es That's love?

J When we encourage others, it is a way of saying we care and we think they are special. One of the most loving things that people can do for each other is to be an encourager.

Es You mean like saying, "okay," "that-a-way," "All right," or "Super Colossal!" *(say with much expression)*

J   You've got it, Es! But it's got to be sincere.

Es   *(holds up card secured to puppet hand)* I got this card from one of my friends at school.

J   How nice. Can I read it?

Es   Sure.

J   *(looks at card and reads)* It says, "Esmerelda, it's not right to say you always have the last word . . ." then inside it says, "it's just that you never get to it!" Happy Valentine's Day.

Es   Now, do you call that encouraging?

J   No, Esmerelda. I just call that fun.

Es   She's right, you know!

J   Shall we pray:
Oh God,
Thank you for Valentine's Day when we can let those around us know what they mean to us. Let us not forget that love is encouraging, helping and just caring. Amen.

MEMORY MEMO
(INFECTION VS. AFFECTION)

HAPPY BIRTHDAY
MERRY CHRISTMAS
CHRIST THE LORD IS RISEN . . .

VALENTINE'S DAY

SINGS: Let Me Call You Sweetheart

CANDY . . . cherries . . . nuts
     -eye strain
     -tooth decay

INFECTION

AFFECTION
     Love . . . Yuck
MORE TO LOVE . . . MEANS CARING ABOUT OTHERS

ENCOURAGEMENT
     -Vent
     -Track Meet
     -Math Whiz
     -Lisa—Hair

OKAY . . . THAT-A-WAY . . .
ALL RIGHT . . .

SUPER COLOSSAL CARD

BEING PREPARED

<u>IDEA:</u> *Beginning of Lent*
<u>PROPS:</u> *Paper attached to hand of puppet*
Pencil behind ear of Ventriloquist

J   Good morning kids, it's wonderful to see you today. *(Turns to Esmerelda)* Hi Es *(turns head back quickly seeing)* Hey, what are you holding?

Es You're 'spose to sign this test. I have to take it back to school tomorrow.

J But you have your hand over the top. Can I see the grade?

Es It's really not important.

J But I WANT to see the grade.

Es You always said it's learning, not marks that count.

J I did say that, but . . . I would like to learn about your mark.

Es You know, Joannie, a grade is really only the teacher's opinion.

J Esmerelda, did you get an F? Or did you get the world's first G?

Es You know what I think? My teacher should've marked this test on the curve.

J I don't care if she marked it on the straight-away. If you don't move your hand . . . I don't sign.

Es *(Slowly lifts her hand)*

J D!

Es It doesn't mean what you think.

J I suppose you're going to tell me this D stands for DEVOTED.

Es I don't think I'd go that far . . . I was DUMBFOUNDED that my grade was so DREADFUL!

J Es, did you study for this test?

Es I studied hard, honestly!

J Then how did you get a D?

Es Well, after I watched my favorite T.V. program, I dug right in and . . . hit the books hard.

J You know Es . . . it really is important to be prepared, no matter what it is.

Es *(hangs head)* Yeah, I guess you're right.

J Today is a really special day, and I want to tell you and all these kids about it.

Es What is it?

J *(Could ask if anyone knows)* Today is the beginning of Lent.

Es Oh, we have lots of that at home.

J *(Looks very confused)* What?

Es Well, we have some under the bed, in the garage, but most of all there is a lot in the clothes dryer.

J ESMERELDA! We aren't talking about LINT, it's LENT!

Es Oh . . . what's LENT?

J It begins on Ash Wednesday and ends on Easter—forty days plus six Sundays.

Es Why 40 days? That's a long time.

J At one time Jesus spent 40 days in the wilderness talking to God, that's the reason for 40 days. Lent means preparing for Easter.

Es So what do we do?

J The church uses the color purple . . . that lets us know Lent is here. And some people give up things for Lent.

Es Really . . . maybe I should give up taking tests.

J We need to give up things we really enjoy.

Es Well, that would have to be Tootsie Rolls . . . I love Tootsie Rolls!

J How much is a Tootsie Roll?

Es The big one is a quarter.

J Then it would be good to put that quarter you would've spent on your favorite candy and give it to something special, like _____ *(a special fund at church or charity)*. You see, Es, when we really give up something and in turn do things for others it really opens us to how Jesus wanted us to live.

Es I get it . . . I could put my quarter in the mission box, for those kids that never get Tootsie Rolls.

J Great idea . . . we all need to prepare our hearts for a wonderful Easter.

Es Hey, Joannie, are you going to sign my test?

J Es, I'll sign it, just promise me next time you will be better prepared.

Es *(Nods head as Joannie takes pencil from ear to sign)* I guess I need to prepare for my test, like we prepare for Easter here at church.

J That's a great idea, Es . . . only one thing . . . you may not have forty days in which to do it! Shall we pray:
Dear God,
Thank you for school, for church, for my family . . . and when I have a task to do, help me to be well prepared. And prepare my heart, God, for this Lenten season. Amen.

MEMORY MEMO
(BEING PREPARED)

PAPER HOLDING
- See Grade
- Learning Not Mark
- Grade—Teacher's Opinion
- D . . . Devoted
- D . . . Dumbfounded, Dreadful

BEING PREPARED
  BEGINNING OF LENT
- under bed
- garage
- clothes dryer

Lent—not Lint

Starts Ash Wednesday—goes 40 days

LENT—Preparing for Easter
- Color Purple
- Give up things—test
-Tootsie Rolls—.25
-Give to others

PREPARE HEARTS FOR EASTER
-Sign test?
-Promise to do better
-May not have 40 days to do it!

DOES GOD LIKE
CHOCOLATE CHIP COOKIES?

IDEA: *When sad or bad things happen in people's lives.*

J Hey, kids, c'mon down. I want you to meet Esmerelda.

Es And I want you to meet Joannie. *(hums a bit)* Hey, while they are coming down I have a joke.

J Esmerelda, you make me very nervous.

Es Don't worry, here goes . . . What is the most common ailment among grapes?

J *(Shrugs Shoulders)* What is the most common ailment among grapes?

Es Cluster-phobia. Here's another one . . . Why did Humpty Dumpty have a great fall?

J I don't know. You know I'm awful at stuff like that!

Es To make up for an awful summer.

J   *(could repeat complete joke with answer as if you didn't get it, to clarify it for the children)* Say, Esmerelda, all the kids are here. Hi kids! Thank goodness, one more of those jokes would've been too much. C'mon Esmerelda, everyone is waiting to hear about your trip.

Es   Wow! Was it ever exciting!

J   Did you go by plane?

Es   Sure did . . . "plain ole boat."

J   Weren't you afraid a storm might come up while you were on the boat?

Es   If it did, I would throw out an anchor.

J   What if a Big storm came up?

Es   I'd throw out a Big anchor.

J   Well, what if a Big, Big storm came up, what would you do?

Es   I'd throw out a Big, Big anchor.

J   *Now wait a minute, Es,* where are you getting all those anchors?

Es   Same place you're getting all those storms!

J   *(thoughtfully)* Esmerelda, what does an anchor do?

Es   Well, it holds the boat safe so it won't dash against the rocks and sink.

J   Esmerelda, you know God is like that.

Es   God is like an anchor?

J   Yes, He reaches out to us and holds us steady through all of life's storms.

Es   What do you mean life's storms?

J   Well the unhappy things that happen to us. Things that make us sad, or make us cry, or make us feel angry because they happened to us. Have you ever felt that way?

Es   Well, I felt really sad . . . awfully sad this year.

J   You did?

Es   *(Sadly)* You see, my gramma, who I loved so much, she died . . . and I really miss her . . . so much. *(Hangs head and looks down)*

J   That would be hard, Esmerelda. *(turning to children)* Have any of you kids had something sad or unhappy happen to you? *(Listen and respond to answers)*

39

J   Esmerelda, how do I explain that sometimes when sad things happen in our lives, that it really can be good . . . You see because a sad thing happens to us, we reach for God, and because of that our lives are better.

Es   I'll explain it!

J   *(surprised)* You will?

Es   You see, it's like this . . . when Gramma was living she hurt so much, that was so sad, but now she's with God, and I know He's taking good care of her, and . . .

J   And what Esmerelda?

Es   I wonder if God likes chocolate chip cookies?

J   What?

Es   Well, Gramma makes the absolute greatest chocolate chip cookies. *(with expression)*

J   *(Hugs Esmerelda)* That's great! I'm sure He does!!!

Es   She used something special in her cookies that made them really, really good.

J   Es, what was that?

Es   Gramma called it "ingredients."

Es   When Gramma was here she would put me to sleep at night and she'd always sing to me.

J   I know she did, Esmerelda.

Es   She sang a song about "GOD WILL TAKE CARE OF YOU."

J   I like that song.

Es   She sang it so often, I don't think I could ever forget it. *(Here puppet could sing the song, or puppet and Vent could take every other line.)*
God will take care of you,
In every way, and all the day.
He will take care of you,
God will take care of you.

J   Thanks, Es *(gives her a hug)*. Thanks for coming up, kids, have a great week.

THE PURPLE GLOVE

<u>IDEA:</u> *We are all the same on the inside*
<u>USAGE:</u> *International Sunday, World Day of Prayer, Mission Sunday or Martin Luther King Sunday.*
<u>PROPS:</u> *Four sewn gloves—purple, yellow, orange and green—made to come off easily*
<u>HINT:</u> *Best done behind a stage with four persons Extremely effective script*

(Narrator reads the following as gloves act it out)

Once upon a time in a busy city, there lived a bright purple gloved hand. He was fun, intelligent and hard working. (*As the words fun, intelligent are read the glove comes to attention with pride*) He could wiggle his fingers and say, "OK." He was a good citizen in his city. (*Wiggle fingers and bring thumb and pointer finger together to form the okay sign.*) He was a very friendly gloved hand and he liked people. He wanted to get to know other gloved hands, so he decided to go out and meet them. (*Purple gloved hand looks both directions and sees other gloved hands coming on stage—yellow, orange, and green*) When the purple gloved hand saw the other gloved hands, he reached out his hand to them, (*hand reaches out as if to shake hands*) but they were not friendly. They thought that he was really weird looking as he wasn't yellow, or green or orange like them. (*Yellow, green and orange move together, excluding the purple gloved hand. Narrator reads each color slowly and as each color is mentioned that color acts haughty and superior*) He certainly would not fit into their group! (*They huddle together on one side of stage—purple on the other*)

They pointed at him (*yellow*) and shook their fists at him (*green*). They pulled away from him. (*orange*) "Bah, stupid purple glove," they said, "get out of here! Ugh, don't let him touch you. He'll poison us all! Run!" (*have green and yellow point, orange pull away using palm in pulling away motion*)

The purple gloved hand felt so terrible he turned his back, slumped down and began to cry. (*purple gloved hand slumps and shakes as if crying*)

The other gloved hands were certainly glad to get rid of him, but they wanted to make sure that he didn't come back, as he wasn't their kind at all, and they wanted to make that very clear, so they huddled together (*green, yellow, and orange come together, wiggle fingers as if talking and planning*) They planned to beat him up and hurt him, so he would certainly understand who was in charge here, and he would never return, and they would be rid of him forever.

Silently and calmly they moved toward the purple gloved hand. (*Sneaking motion with fingers down*) Suddenly they pounced on the unsuspecting purple gloved hand with quick sudden movements. *(Narrator becomes excited as he reads)*

With a loud blow and a wallop they pounded the poor purple gloved hand. With a clenched fist they sent blow after blow, they knocked him to the ground, when he got up they would strike again, then a merciless upper-cut that sent him reeling again. In all the commotion and hassle they pulled the purple glove right off his hand! *(This part has much action, green poking with pointer finger, and orange could come in with the upcut blow. Plan which glove should pull the glove off the hand and when that happens the purple gloved hand could tremble with fear, and drop to the ground in a ball—the back of hand facing the others)*

The yellow, orange, and green gloved hands were so surprised at what happened that they pulled back in utter shock. *(Have orange, yellow, green pull back with fingers wide open in total surprise)* They looked at each other, the yellow glove removed the green glove, the green removed the orange glove, and the orange took off the yellow glove. They looked back at the hand they had hit and bashed . . . why, they were all the same on the inside! There was hardly any difference at all! *(Hands turn front and back as if looking at self in a mirror.)*

Gently and tenderly the hands came together as friends do. *(At this point one hand could tap on the back of the purple gloved hand that is curled to one side of the stage still hovering in fear. With that tap, the purple gloved hand rises and turns and comes slowly, carefully, suspiciously toward the others. Fingers touch gently. Maybe a pat on the back)* They realized each one was okay, one of God's children, a part of the world, but most of all they needed each other. God had given each one gifts to be shared. They shook hands and hoped that maybe their friendship might make a small difference in a big world. *(As narrator says "okay" have one hand make the okay sign with the thumb and pointer finger curled; as the narrator says "part of the world," have a hand make a sweeping motion, palm up; and as the narrator says: "needed each other" have a hand give the thumbs up motion, followed by a repeat thumbs up by remaining hands. Then have hands shake hands. You will need two right hands and two left hands to do this. Hands exit in up-lifting movements to music if desired)*

CLOSING SONG: Red, Brown, Yellow, Black and White
                They are precious in His sight,
                Jesus loves the little children,
                Of the world.

FAITH IN OUR GOD

IDEA: *Faith and Trust in God—(based on Gen. 12:1-8)*
PROP: *Seeds*

J   Good Morning, boys and girls. It is very nice to see you. Do you all remember Esmerelda?

Es   Hi, Kids! Gosh, don't they look great? *(sniffing)* What's that I smell?

J   It's my new cologne. Isn't it great? It's called "Evening in London." It sells for $20 an ounce. *(Pause, sniffs near figure—noticing her cologne)* What's that you're wearing?

Es   It's called Evening in _____ *(give name of your town)* and it sells for $5 a gallon.

J   Okay, okay, you have the introduction this morning, remember?

Es   Okie, Dokie . . . here goes. Today, we would like to share a little routine that we performed for President _____ *(President of the country)*

J   Esmerelda, quit exaggerating!

Es   It's true. At our last performance I heard an old man in the front row say, "If that girl is a ventriloquist . . . then I'm _____" *(President of United States)*

J   *(Pause—looking very dejected)*

Es   Did I say something wrong?

J   Esmerelda . . . yes, you certainly did say something wrong.

Es   I'm sorry, I was . . . *(Joannie closes puppet's mouth)*

J   Do you know what faith means?

Es   Faith?

J   Yeah, faith. I had faith in you and you sorta' let me down.

Es   I did? I'm sorry. *(hangs head)*

J   It's okay. I still like you. I never know what you are going to say, but I still like you. In the scripture today we read about Abraham leaving his country and moving his family, but he had faith in God that it would work out.

Es   Do you think he was scared?

J   Maybe he was. He didn't know what was ahead, but he trusted God. Have any of you kids ever moved? *(acknowledge those)* Were you scared? Or worried to leave your friends? *(Wait for answers after questions) (Be sure puppet faces each child as they answer.)* But your mom or dad said it would be okay and you trusted them, you had faith in them.

Es   This morning when we came to church . . .

J   Yes . . .

Es   The grass is brown, the trees are brown . . . but I know God will change it to green. We all have faith Spring will come . . . it always does . . . absolutely amazing!

J   It sure is, Esmerelda. *(to children)* Do you see what I have in my hand? *(hand open holding seeds)* Children, what do you see? *(answer "Seeds")* Esmerelda, what do you see?

Es   A dead plant!

J   You always see things a bit differently, don't you, Esmerelda? These are seeds.

Es   Well, it's dead until you put it in the ground and God sends rain and warm sun . . . then it comes alive and grows into flowers or corn or tomatoes.

J   I like that!

Es   You do?

J   Yeah, that's good. And we need to have faith that God takes our discouraged, dead, downhearted lives and makes them come alive too . . . like the seed. If only we could draw our faith and strength from God more often . . . if we could trust him more.

Es   Well . . . if God can bring life to dead seeds every year, I know he wants to bring new life to us.

J   You are so right, Esmerelda. At least we should have as much faith as this seed of corn!
Shall we pray:
Dear God,
Thank you so much for trees that change from brown to green; for seeds that change into flowers; and may we too change and grow to have a stronger faith in You.
Amen.

J   Thanks so much, kids. Have a wonderful week.

MEMORY MEMO
(FAITH IN GOD)

COLOGNE

ROUTINE FOR PRESIDENT

FAITH
- Abraham leaving his country
- scared
- trusted God
- trusted parents

TRUST GOD
- Spring will come

SEEDS—"dead plant"
- Sun
- Rain
- Flowers or "tomatoes"

GOD BRINGS NEW LIFE TO US

DRAW FAITH AND STRENGTH FROM GOD

*IF GOD BRINGS LIFE TO DEAD SEEDS—CAN
   BRING NEW LIFE TO US*

PRAYER

WHAT IS A SAINT?

IDEA: *St. Patrick's Day*
PROPS: *Puppet wearing green*
A green shamrock

J Esmerelda, Good Morning! You have exactly the right color on today.
(Esmerelda is dressed mostly in green)

Es I do?

J Yes, it's just perfect.

Es Perfect for what?

J Well, do you know what special day took place this week?

Es *(Esmerelda drops head and thinks)* Let's see, on Wednesday it rained again
. . . I think God had us on the rinse cycle . . . *(or use weather of your area)*

J No, Es, nothing to do with weather

Es On Thursday someone took my lunch . . .

J No, really?

Es It had my favorite candy bar . . .

J That's awful . . .

Es And peanut butter and jelly sand . . .

J *(interrupts)* Es, it has nothing to do with food!

Es Joannie, just where are we going with all of this? I really don't have the slightest idea what you are talking about.

J Remember I said you were wearing the perfect color . . .

Es Yep . . . *(looks down at dress)* Green, you said . . . Oh, "Wearin' of the Green."

J You're getting close . . St. Patrick's Day.

Es I have a friend named Patrick . . . but he's no saint! *(looks at Joannie)* What is a saint, Joannie?

J Well, Es, a saint is someone who is thought to be very special. A patron saint takes special care of a country or group. The Irish believe that Saint Patrick watches over them.

Es What if you're not Irish . . . then what?

J People all over the world celebrate St. Patrick's Day—even those that aren't Irish. You see he was a good person.

Es Can you tell me about him?

J Patrick wasn't from Ireland.

Es *(surprise)* He wasn't?

J He was from Britain. When he was a young boy he was kidnapped and brought to Ireland and made a slave.

Es Oh, no!

J His master made him herd sheep. He prayed often to God to help him and six years later he escaped and he went back to Britain.

Es Holy Cow, six years away from home. I'll bet he never went back to Ireland again.

J Well, Es, he thought a lot and prayed a lot and he finally realized what he wanted to do.

Es I bet it wasn't herding sheep!

J Well, in a way, maybe you could call it that.

Es You're kidding me!

J He wanted to return to Ireland and teach people about God. So you see the Irish people were the sheep. He studied hard and eventually the head of the Catholic Church, the Pope, named him Patricius, Latin for Patrick.

Es So then what did he do?

J He sailed to Ireland, he built churches and schools. He was a kind and loving person, the people trusted him. He spent his whole life caring for the Irish people. They loved this kind man very much. That's why the Catholic Church made him a saint.

Es What's all this have to do with green?

J In the month of March people in Ireland gathered green leaves and branches and burned them. Then they spread the ashes in the fields to make them green and fertile. You see to wear green is to honor Ireland, the Emerald Isle.

Es Wow, I didn't even know I was honoring a country.

J People have lots of fun on St. Patrick's Day. They have parades and send cards. They share cookies and cakes, often with green frosting.

Es Yummmmmm.

J They wear green, like you, and others wear green carnations. They have parties and sing Irish songs and dance Irish jigs. And most everyone wears a green shamrock.

Es A green shamrock? What is that?

J Well, it looks like this. *(take out 3-leafed shamrock)*

Es What's that got to do with Saint Patrick?

J The story is told that one day Saint Patrick was trying to explain to people about the Holy Trinity. They didn't seem to be understanding. Growing at his feet was a shamrock . . . this *(hold paper shamrock so all can see)* He picked it and pointed to each leaf—one God in three divine beings, the Father, the Son and the Holy Spirit. He used this plant to explain three in one, one stem with three leaves.

Es That's really neat. And even if I'm not Irish—I guess I sorta' feel Irish on March 17th—St. Patrick's Day!

J Guess we all do. Do you 'spose you could have o' bit of Irish in you . . . or maybe someone just liked the color green.

Es *(looks at her green body)* Well, Joannie, even if I'm not Irish, I would like to be like St. Patrick. He was kind, he cared about others and people trusted him and most of all . . . God was his friend.

J How right you are, Es . . . shall we pray.
Dear God,
Thank you for special people like St. Patrick who loved you enough to share You with others. May we learn to care and love others as St. Patrick did.   Amen.

MEMORY MEMO
(WHAT IS A SAINT?)

COLOR GREEN
SPECIAL DAY
   Wed—rained
   Thurs—took lunch

St. Patrick's Day
What is—Saint?

Irish believe—watches over them

St. Patrick
  - From Britain
    - Kidnapped
    - Returned Ireland—teach about God
    - Built churches and schools
    - Kind, loving person

St. Patrick explains Holy Trinity
   - Shamrock
Like to be like St. Patrick
   - Kind
   - Cared
   - Trusted
   - God was his friend

"I HATE BOOTS!"

IDEA: *Frustrations (this script for young children)*
Everyone feels frustrated sometime. To help children accept disappointment.
PROP: *Puppet could wear boots.*

Es Hey, Joannie, why is winter the best time to buy a thermometer?

J Why is winter the best time to buy a thermometer? Boy, you got me!

Es Well, they are a lot higher in the summer.

J I should've gotten that one—but isn't the snow pretty? Everything is so crisp and white.

Es If the house gets all covered with snow, does that mean we'll all be under the weather?

J   *(laughs)* Not really, Es.

Es   Winter may be nice, but some things I don't like at all.

J   What's that?

Es   Like boots and mittens.

J   You don't like boots and mittens? They sure are handy in the winter.

Es   Yesterday I was going out to play with my friends. I put on my hat—my scarf—my snowpants and my coat. By the time I got all that on I almost forgot where I was going.

J   Then what?

Es   Well, I tried to put the left boot on the right foot. But that didn't fit. So then I tried to put the right boot on the left foot, and that didn't fit either. So I threw the boot.

J   You were frustrated!

Es   What?

J   Frustrated—it means angry, upset.

Es   Boy, was I frustrated! And angry and upset too. And that wasn't all.

J   There's more?

Es   Yep, my mitten, the thumb got my little finger . . . It didn't work. I started to cry. I didn't even know if I wanted to go outside anymore.

J   Let me show you a good rule, Esmerelda. Put the boots together *(have a pair to demo)* and buckles or buttons always go on the "outside." See. And a good rule for mittens *(again show children)* is the thumb is always on the "inside." *Maybe have a child do this for others to see)*

Es   I think I got it now! But your song helped me the most.

J   Shall we teach it to them? You sing it for them.

Es   *(Song: tune of Row, Row, Row Your Boat)*
Boots, Boots, put them on
Buckles outside go,
Do this every single time,
It's a handy thing to know.
(Could go over it a few times with children)

J   Let's teach them the mitten one too, Es.

Es   Mittens, Mittens put them on,
         Thumbs inside go,
         Do this every single time
         It's a handy thing to know.
         (again could go over a few times)

J   Can you think of other times you've been frustrated?

Es   Boy, can I ever . . . once I couldn't reach the cookie jar, I couldn't get
         my pop can open and one time I couldn't find my other shoe and Dad
         was honking the horn to go to school.

J   Esmerelda, do you know that everyone gets frustrated sometimes, even
         adults?

Es   You do? Do you have trouble getting your boots on?

J   Maybe not that, but . . .

Es   But what?

J   Things that frustrate me are long lines, telephone calls at dinnertime,
         rush hour traffic, high prices and kids who don't pick up their rooms.

Es   Who, me?

J   When we get frustrated we need to stop and see how we can solve it or
         accept the disappointment. But most of all we shouldn't make others
         unhappy because of how we are feeling.

Es   Everyone around me knows how I feel. I don't hide it very well. I need
         to do better on that one.

J   I like your honesty, Es.

Es   Here's a good two-liner:
         When you're frustrated and mad,
         Don't make others feel sad.

J   I like it, Esmerelda. Shall we pray.
         Dear God,
         When we get angry and frustrated, help us to work it out. May we
         think how we make others feel. You are there to help us and love us.
         Thank you, Lord.
         Amen.

MEMORY MEMO

RIDDLE: Thermometer
  - Under the weather

DON'T LIKE BOOTS AND MITTENS
THREW THE BOOT
  Frustrated—angry . . . upset
MITTENS
  Thumb in little finger

Rule for boots—buckles always on outside
Rule for mittens—Thumb always on the inside

SONG

OTHER FRUSTRATIONS
  - cookie jar
  - pop can
  - shoe

DON'T MAKE OTHERS UNHAPPY
  When you're frustrated and mad
  Don't make other people sad.

PRAYER

PALM SUNDAY

Es   Good morning, kids. Boy, do you look great. What a HANDY group of kids we have here.

J   They sure do look nice, Es.

Es   This morning in church I told the usher that I would help him pass out the bulletins. He said he needed a right-hand-man . . . er . . . girl.

J   Did you help him?

Es   Nope.

J   Well, how come?

Es   I'm left-handed.

J   Es!

Es   Joannie, give me your hand. *(Joannie puts hand in puppet's lap. Top of hand up)*

Es   No, turn it over.

J   What's all this hand business, Esmerelda?

Es   I'm going to read your palm.

J   Read my palm? What on earth for?

51

Es Joannie . . . just listen. *(looking at palm)* See this line here that starts at the wrist and goes up here and then stops?

J What's that mean?

Es It means you're at the end of your rope.

J Well . . . sometimes . . . you DO create situations that cause me to feel that way.

Es *(continues and points)* See this wide curve, and this wide curve, and here's another wide curve . . . and see they all come together here.

J So what does that mean?

Es *(looks confused)* I dunno . . . I think they need a turn signal here.

J C'mon, Es.

Es And see up here, these bumps . . . this is a mountain range.

J I'm sorry, Esmerelda, but those are callouses . . . I work hard!

Es *(continues talking and pointing)* This gold band here . . . signifies "there is gold in them thar' hills."

J That's my ring . . . listen, enough of this foolishness—why all this palm reading anyway?

Es Well, Joannie, you know this is Palm Sunday . . . so I thought . . .

J You thought that it had to do with our palm *(holds up hand)*. Es, Palm Sunday doesn't have anything to do with the palm of our hand.

Es It doesn't?

J No, it was a very special day when Jesus rode into Jerusalem.

Es I don't get it. Why do they call it Palm Sunday? *(holds up hand)*

J You see, Es, Jesus' followers borrowed a donkey so that Jesus could ride into the city, and as he rode there was great shouting and cheering and excitement!

Es *(still looks confused)*

J Many took off their robes and laid them in front of the donkey, and others broke off branches of the palm tree and laid them in his path.

Es Palm trees?

J   Yes. You see, it was their way of welcoming him, of saying we love you . . .
you are our King.

Es   *(says slowly)* So . . . Palm Sunday has to do with palm trees . . .and
shouting and excitement . . . and a donkey and a huge crowd and . . .
J   And people shouting Hosanna!

Es   Boy, that IS exciting . . . much more exciting than the palm of your hand.

J   I guess I would certainly agree with that.

Es   Joannie, may I make a suggestion?

J   Certainly.

Es   Hand lotion and gloves do wonders for bumpy hands.

J   Esmerelda! Shall we pray:
God, we thank you for this glorious day when Jesus rode into Jerusalem.
May he ride into our hearts and be with us through this week, helping
us to be kind, caring and helpful. Amen.

MEMORY MEMO
(PALM SUNDAY)

RIGHT HAND MAN
READ PALM
PALM SUNDAY
- nothing to do with reading palm
- day Jesus rode into Jerusalem
- Robes and palm branches
- Excitement—donkey—huge crowd
- Hosanna
HAND LOTION AND GLOVES
PRAYER

EMPTY OR FULL
(LET EASTER HAPPEN TO YOU)

Es   Wow, look at this place! It's beautiful! Gold . . . white lilies, lots of people
. . . wow!

J   This is such a great Sunday, Es.

Es   *(looks over crowd)* Holy Cow, it must be a real celebration, and nobody
wanted to miss it!

J   The music, the people, the feeling of excitement . . . no, I don't think anyone would want to miss it.

Es   But Joannie, this was a very sad week, *(slowly and sadly)* they hung Jesus on a cross, and he died, then they put him in a tomb and rolled a big rock in front of it. Jesus' friends and followers . . . well, they had never been so sad.

J   Yes, it was a very sad time . . . that Easter long ago, Mary Magdalene, one of Jesus' friends, went to the tomb and when she got there, the stone had been rolled away. She cried out, "Someone has stolen my Lord!"

Es   *(surprised)* What happened?

J   Jesus wasn't there . . . the tomb was EMPTY!

Es   Really?

J   Mary Magdalene was devastated seeing that EMPTY tomb. Have you noticed how often when things are empty we think it's bad? What are some empty things you don't like?

Es   An empty billfold is terrible!

J   Anyone else? *(call on kids here)*
Some things you might get or encourage:
- Empty mailbox
- Empty milk carton
- Empty cereal box
- Empty house

Es   An empty gas tank is really the pits!

J   How right you are!

Es   And Joannie, you know what else, sometimes I feel empty inside . . . like when my gramma died . . . I felt like something awful was missing.

J   *(Gently)* I know . . . I'm sure that is the way Jesus' friends felt, so empty, so lost, not knowing what to do.

Es   I guess they wanted to get rid of that empty feeling.

J   What do you do, Esmerelda, when things are empty—like your billfold?

Es   Well, I guess I need to get a job, so I can fill it back up again.

J   What about an empty mailbox?

Es   Well, I guess I could write some letters, then I'd get some mail.

J What about that empty feeling inside. *(points to body)*

Es I guess I could do something for others, then I would feel better.

J *(Emphasize)* You see, Es, when things are empty it makes us want to refill. It motivates us to get going, to make changes.

Es I see.

J Esmerelda, the tomb was empty . . . but Christ had risen . . . there was joy . . . not emptiness.

Es Maybe that's why we are all here, to FILL UP!

J I think so, Es. It's a new beginning, a chance to put the hope of Easter in our hearts.

Es WOW! I hope Easter happens to me.

J Shall we pray:
O God:
We thank you for this glorious Easter morning. May we not be afraid of emptiness, but fill us with the joy and hope of this day and may we carry it in our hearts. Amen.
Wish all a Happy Easter!

MEMORY MEMO
(EMPTY OR FULL)

Es WOW—Gold-white

J Great Sunday

Es real celebration—Nobody miss it

J Music—People—Feeling excitement

Es sad week: Jesus cross—died—tomb—friends

J Sad Easter . . . M. Mag . . . "Someone stole my Lord"

J Tomb—empty
   - When empty-think it's bad
   - What are some empty things you don't like?

Es Empty billfold

J Else? *(Ask children)*
Following suggestions: Chance to put the hope of Easter in heart
Empty mailbox—Empty milk carton—Empty house

55

Es Empty gas tank—pits!
Gramma died—empty

J What do—when things are empty—billfold

Es Job—fill billfold—Write letters—Empty feeling—do for others

J When things are empty it makes us want to refill. It motivates us to get going, to make changes.

Es I see

J Tomb empty—Christ risen—Joy . . . not emptiness.

Es Why here—to FILL UP!

J New beginning—Chance to put the hope of Easter in heart

HE'S A KING!

IDEA: *What is a King? Walk to Emmaus.*
PROP: *If have picture of "Walk to Emmaus" could use it.*

Es No more "Hosanna to Our King" or "King of the Jews" . . . I'm sorta' sad Easter is over. I guess the disciples were pretty sad too, huh, Joannie?

J Yes, Es, they had lost their King, their friend and leader; they were confused . . . you see, Es, they saw in Jesus the possibility of a new life and hope . . . and now he was gone.

Es I 'spose it was like when Mrs. Nelson lost her husband . . .

J How do you mean?

Es She said . . . she kept thinking he'd walk thru the door. And one time she said it seemed like he was sitting in his favorite chair.

J Let me tell you about the Walk to Emmaus.

Es Emmaus?

J That's a town, and two of the disciples were walking the dusty road, talking about all the things that had happened in Jerusalem.

Es You mean about Jesus being crucified?

J   Yes, Es, they were very sad and suddenly a stranger joined them. It seemed he had not heard about all that had happened. They could not understand that this stranger had not heard.

Es   Did they tell him?

J   Yes, and they felt his kind and gentle spirit. When they got to Emmaus, it was getting dark, so they asked him to eat with them.

Es   They did?

J   Es, when they sat down to eat this stranger blessed the bread and broke it and gave it to them . . . all of a sudden they knew him!

Es   It was Jesus, wasn't it?

J   Yes, they had felt something so different as they had walked like he was right there with them.

Es   But how could he be, Joannie? He had died.

J   Es, remember how you said Mrs. Nelson felt her husband was in his favorite chair, even after he had died? She felt like he was right there with her.

Es   I see, it's something you feel . . . but why did they call him a King, Joannie?

J   Esmerelda, tell me, what is a king?

Es   Well, he's very rich . . .

J   Jesus was poor.

Es   A king lives in a palace . . .

J   Jesus walked among the people.

Es   A king has servants and maids . . .

J   Jesus had common ordinary disciples.

Es   A king wears a crown with jewels . . .

J   Jesus wore a crown of thorns.

Es   A king has armies and chariots to go to war . . .

J   Jesus preached love and peace.

Es Well, Joannie, a king has beautiful flowing robes . . .

J Jesus was very simply dressed.

Es Was he really a king?

J He certainly was a different kind of king, Esmerelda. He didn't just tell people what to do, like most kings. He reached out to the poor, the children, healed the sick. He gave people hope, and a chance to live a better life. He didn't come to be served, he came to serve.

Es Wow! No wonder everyone loved him, he CERTAINLY was a different kind of king.

J Shall we pray:
Dear God:
Thank you for giving us Jesus . . . for his love, caring and kindness. Make us disciples too, that we might follow this very rare and uncommon king. Amen.

MEMORY MEMO
(HE'S A KING)

NO MORE HOSANNA—disciples sad

LOST KING—friend, leader

JESUS—possibility of new life and hope—gone
Mrs. Nelson

WALK TO EMMAUS
- two disciples
- talked about Jerusalem
- Jesus crucified
- stranger joined them

EMMAUS
-asked stranger to join them
-stranger blessed bread—broke it
-all sudden—knew Him

A DIFFERENT KIND OF KING
- Reached out to poor
- Healed sick
- Gave people hope

CERTAINLY was a different King!

HOW COULD IT BE?
- Like Mrs. Nelson
- Something you feel

WHY CALLED KING?
- Rich
- Palace
- Servants
- Crown, jewels
- Armies, War
- Beautiful robes

JESUS
-Poor
-Walked among people
-Common disciples
-Crown of thorns
-Preached peace
-Simply dressed

LOST LAMB
(LUKE 15:3-7)

<u>IDEA:</u> *Story of the Lost Lamb*
<u>PROPS:</u> *Horoscope from Newspaper*

J   Esmerelda, I didn't know if we'd ever get to church on time today; you certainly were not very automatic this morning.

Es   I was tired. I guess I wasn't very automatic, but we sure live in an automated society.

J   What is that 'spose to mean?

Es   Did you notice on the way to church when a traffic signal turns green it automatically activated the horn of the car behind us?

J   *(laughs)* Come to think of it . . . you're right. But it's finally getting nicer. I sure don't like driving in all that snow.

Es   I like the snow, but that shovel, shovel, shovel . . . why can't we get a snowblower? We must be the only family on the block that still shovels the driveway by hand!

J   It builds character, Esmerelda.

Es   Pretty convenient how every time I build character, she saves a few hundred bucks!

J   *(looks exasperated—then notices paper in figure's hand)* Say, what do you have there?

Es   This was in _____ *(name of local newspaper)*. I'm trying to figure it out.

J   Let's see *(looks at paper)* Oh, Esmerelda, this is a horoscope.

Es   Horoscope? I thought a horoscope was a kissing sweet mouthwash.

J   Funny, Es. A horoscope has nothing to do with mouthwash.

Es   What is it, then?

J   Well, see, it's like this . . . *(points to paper)* You look up your birthday and the horoscope tells you your future and what's going to happen to you.

Es   That's real neat, huh?

J   Esmerelda, have you got your head on backwards?

Es I . . . I . . . I . . . don't think so. *(moves head as if to check)* It was okay when I left.

J I mean . . . you don't really believe that stuff, do you?

Es Let's see *(looks at paper)* It says, I'm going to meet a handsome man. Yuck!

J Well, anyway, I hope he likes green. *(or color of puppet)*

Es What?

J Nothing.

Es Also it says money and love are in my future. Hey, cool!

J Don't believe everything that you read. Some of it is just a lot of phoney bologna!

Es Maybe it's true, Joannie.

J Esmerelda, you don't need a horoscope to tell you about love. We just need to read the Bible and learn more about Jesus and the kind of love he tried to share with us.

Es I don't get it.

J Jesus once told the story of the Good Shepherd who had taken his flock out to pasture. It was spring and the sun was warm and the grass was green. To this one little lamb the green grass probably looked greener in the distance and he wandered further and further away.

Es Kinda' like when we went to the mall and you said, "Esmerelda, if you don't stay right here you'll just have to go sit in the car."

J *(rather embarrassed)* Did I say that?

Es You sure did!

J Well . . . as I was saying . . . the little lamb must've reached for some grass on a cliff, because he slipped and tumbled and got stuck in a thorny bush.

Es Oh, no, how awful!

J He was bruised, the thorns hurt, and as it got dark he worried about the wolves. He cried "baaaaaa" as loud as he could, but no one heard him.

Es Didn't the Good Shepherd miss him?

J   Well, Es, the shepherd had 100 sheep.

Es   That's a lot.

J   Yes, it is, and as he was putting them in the fold for the night he was counting . . . 97, 98, 99 . . . number 100 was gone . . .missing.

Es   Number 100 was gone . . . so did he go look for him?

J   He sure did! He headed out in the dark calling and calling, and when he heard the little lamb bleating he followed the sound, and the shepherd leaned far out over the cliff, he hooked the shepherd's crook around the little lamb, and with his strong arms pulled the little lamb to safety.

Es   Was Jesus trying to tell us that God is like that?

J   I really think so, Esmerelda . . . you see, many times we too wander away from the flock, but God misses us and comes looking for us.

Es   You mean he loves us even when we stray away from Him?

J   You bet he does, Es. Isn't it a wonderful feeling to know that when we are lost, a gentle God reaches down and picks us up?

Es   Wow! That kind of love sure is better than any old horoscope!

J   It sure is. Shall we pray:
Dear God,
Thank you so much for coming to look for us when we stray . . . for loving us . . . and for keeping us safe in your arms.
Amen.

MEMORY MEMO
(THE LOST LAMB)

TRAFFIC SIGNAL

SHOVEL

HOROSCOPE—mouthwash
- handsome man
- money
- love

STORY—GOOD SHEPHERD
- We also wander away from flock—God misses us
- When we are lost—God reaches down—picks us up
- Better than any old horoscope

PRAYER

MOM'S RESUMÉ

IDEA: *Mother's Day*
PROP: *Resumé*

Es OK, Joannie, here's one for you . . . What did the baby corn say to the mommy corn?

J What "did" baby corn say to mommy corn?

Es Where's popcorn?

J Really, Es!

Es Try this one . . . what did the digital clock say to its mother?

J *(Sigh)* Let's hear it.

Es Look, Ma, no hands!

J I guess I've heard that a few times. But listen, Es, I have a question for you . . . Do you know what a resumé is?

Es Do I know what a Resumé is? "(thinks a bit)" Well . . . is it like when I ask if I can go to the movies and I'm REALLY surprised 'cuz you say 'EZ-U-MAY.'

J *(Repeats)* Resumé . . . Ez-U-May . . . no, this has nothing to do with that at all. *(explains)* You see, a Resumé is a list of all the things you do well. And if you want to get a job, you make out this RESUMÉ and give it to the person you want to work for and . . .

Es I get it . . . You're going to tell us all the things that you do well.

J Not too many people are standing in line for this job, but this list or resumé pretty much tells what we mothers do.

Es Ok . . . shoot!
(much of the following could be read—eliminating need for memorization)

J *(Clear throat)* . . . Resumé of a Mother: Fully qualified as chauffeur, cook, social director, laundress . . .

Es What's that?

J A laundress is the person who does the wash . . . *(continues)* she's a bookkeeper and a bank. There is no salary, health plan, or vacation days. She works seven days a week and holidays.

Es Doesn't sound like a job I'd like to have.

J (Continues)
- She can thaw hamburger in the dry cycle of the dishwasher and use it in 27 different ways.
- She can dress naked dolls.
- Take phone messages for those who have a social life.
- She plays cards with sick kids who cheat.
- She can make Christmas ornaments out of just about anything.
- She can make cookies in heart shapes for Valentines, Turkeys for Thanksgiving and stars for Christmas, and they taste wonderful.
- She keeps kids from killing each other.
- Wipes noses and fannies and kisses bloody knees.
- She checks the refrigerator for rotten food.
- She eats lunches that would be thrown out anyway.
- She teaches honesty and manners like "Please" and "Thank-you."
- She spends days on a lawn chair at Little League games—sometimes in the rain.
- AND SHE . . . DRIVES . . . DRIVES . . . DRIVES . . . AND DRIVES!

Es Holy Cow! . . . And I remember the time I called you at work . . . remember the time you were in the middle of an important meeting . . . and I called to see what we were having for dinner?

J I sure do . . . it was kinda' like calling 911 because the dog threw up!

Es It's too hard being a mom . . . I don't think I'm gonna be one.

J You know, Es, moms keep being moms because lots of good things happen too.

Es Joannie, remember when you went to that early morning Bible Study and Dad was 'spose to get us dressed, fed and to school?

J I sure remember . . . you were all late.

Es We didn't want to get marked late, so we had Dad write us a note.

J So how did he explain that one?

Es He just wrote "Please excuse this lateness. Our power went out early this morning!"

J Interesting . . . Shall we pray:
Dear God:
To be moms, we need that special power that comes from you. May we possess the love you have shown us, and share it with these special children. Amen.

Comment on leaving: Wish your Mom a very Happy Mother's Day.

MEMORY MEMO
(MOTHER'S RESUMÉ)

BABY CORN—POPCORN

DIGITAL CLOCK—NO HANDS

DO YOU KNOW WHAT RESUMÉ IS?
- Es-u-may
- all things you do well

MAKE LIST AND READ: (resume' for mom)
CALLED - WHAT FOR DINNER
-911 - DOG
-being mom—too hard—not going
to be one

Dad 'spose to get us up—Power went out

THE SOWER
SCRIPTURE MARK 4:1-9

Es *(Singing)* Holy, holy, holy . . . Lord God almighty . . .

J Esmerelda . . . please . . . shhhhhhhh

Es (continues singing) Early in the morning our . . .

J Esmerelda, we have the children's sermon . . . we are not in the choir!

Es *(still singing)* . . . song shall rise to . . . we do?

J You know that we do, we talked it over . . . you know the scripture about the Sower and the seeds. That's our subject today.

Es Ya mean _____ *(name of minister)* is out of a job today?

J We might be out of a job unless you settle down.

Es Speaking of Rev. _____, I was in his office the other day, and he has a special file for his bills . . . It's labeled DUE UNTO OTHERS.

J ESMERELDA! You shouldn't be looking at the Pastor's files!

Es While I was in there he was working on his sermon, and I said, "Pastor _____ does the Lord tell you what to say?

J What did he say?

Es He said, "Well, of course He does!" So then I asked him why he kept scratching some of it out!

J *(clears throat)* I want to know what you got out of the scripture this morning . . . the scripture about the Sower planting his seeds.

Es Well, if you want your seeds to grow, be very sure they don't land on the path, the rocks or in the thorns.

J Hey, I'm impressed! Tell me, what happens if the seeds land in the path?

Es You see, the birds swoop down and eat them.

J Good. Now what happens if they land on the rock?

Es Well, there isn't much soil so when the sun comes out it dries them all up, 'cuz the root has nowhere to go.

J That's right. Then what happens if they land in the thorns?

Es Hey, what is this? Twenty questions?

J Okay, I'll answer this one . . . when the plant starts growing in the thorns, the thorns grow up around it and choke out the plant.

Es Joannie, is this a lesson on gardening?

J No, Esmerelda, Jesus said that we were a lot like those seeds.

Es He did? I don't get it!

J Okay, Esmerelda, let's pretend that you are in Sunday School and your teacher is going to tell you how very much Jesus loves each of us.

Es Yeah, I got it!

J Okay, picture your class. The teacher is telling about Jesus' love and one of the kids is playing with an airplane that he brought to class and he DOESN'T HEAR A WORD SHE SAYS.

Es I got it, like the seed that falls on the path. The birds eat it and it never even gets a chance to grow.

J You are so right! Then there is another boy who's twirling his pencil around his finger. He hears a little bit, but soon he's into the pencil and doesn't hear much.

Es Like the seeds that fall on the rock, they get started, but die. They don't make it, do they?

J No, Es. Okay, there is another girl over there in class and she is talking to all her friends. She's really into all that happened at school . . . The cutest boy . . .

Es *(Expressive!)* Tell me about it! That has to be Helen Ander . . .

J   *(Puppeteer covers mouth of puppet)* No names please!

Es   I see, she's like the seed that falls into thorns. The seed gets choked out by the thorns . . . like she is choked out by all her friends, and she doesn't hear what the teacher says.

J   But then, Esmerelda, there are those who listen and hear what the teacher says about God's love, and their roots go deep like the seeds in good soil, and the plant comes up strong and can stand tall because they are rooted deep in their faith.

Es   Wow! I bet _____ *(Pastor's name)* can't top that!

J   *(Smiles)* Shall we pray:
Dear God:
Thank you for a chance to grow and become something special in your world. May our roots go deep and may we stand strong. Amen.

MEMORY MEMO
(THE SOWER)

HOLY, HOLY
- Sower
- Preacher (name)
- Due unto others—file
- does Lord tell what to say?

WHAT GOT OUT OF SCRIPTURE?
- very sure don't land—path—rock—thorns
- path—birds
- rock—sun dries
- thorns—choke

PRETEND—SUNDAY SCHOOL
- listen—hear
- roots go deep—seeds in good soil

STAND AGAINST LIFE'S STORMS

ROOTED DEEP IN FAITH

DANIEL AND THE LION

IDEA: *Esmerelda writes a play in Sunday School*
Hint: *Little preparation—could be read*
PROP: *Script*

(Script is in Esmerelda's hand)

J   What have you got in your hand?

Es   It's a script. Our teacher had us write one in Sunday School.

J   Really . . . what about?

Es Well, we have been studying about Daniel in the Lion's Den.

J That's interesting . . . tell me about Daniel.

Es Well, he's the one that kept praying to his God even when they told him not to . . . so they dumped him in the Lion's Den.

J So you wrote a script about it?

Es Yep, so I want you to help me with it . . . I'll be Daniel and you be the lion.

J You mean the lion has a speaking part? *(looks at script)*

Es In this play he does . . . you start . . . read the directions first.

J Okay . . . here goes. Puppet comes hurling over the top of the stage, then lands with a crash and thud, sounds of struggling. Daniel says, "Ouch," and snarls heard from lions. *(Joannie looks at Esmerelda)* . . . Daniel says "Ouch?"

Es Yeh, the lion speaks first . . . that's you.

J Holy Cow, watch where you are going! Look what you did . . . you messed up my gorgeous mane.

Es You are 'spose to roar when you say that.

J Roar? It doesn't say so on the script.

Es So . . . I forgot to write it . . . let's see, my turn . . . Oh, pardon me. How can you see anything, it's so dark and damp down here?

J *(finding place in script)* Oh, Lion speaks . . . Boy, you sure have the nerve . . . come flying in here and start complaining about the accommodations.

Es Wow, you look sorta' fierce . . . unfriendly . . . wild and scary . . . I think I'll leave.

J Sorry, there's only one way out . . . and that's the same way you came in . . . *(points up with pointer finger)*

Es When was your last meal? Are you hungry? Have they starved you? Are you going to eat me?

J What are you anyway, a reporter?

Es Not really.

J Then why the survey?

Es Well . . . I just thought . . .

J Well, don't worry about us getting hungry. We're all on a diet down here.

Es A diet?

J Yeh, we kinda' got special orders . . . via Federal Express.

Es Federal Express!

J I'm just reading what it says here . . . the orders said we weren't to touch he next guy that they threw in . . . we do and we're outta' here.

Es Well, wouldn't that be okay . . . to split?

J Not really . . . we get three squares around here . . . can't beat that! *(looks at Esmerelda questioning—looking at script)* Is this for real? Where did you come up with all this?

Es Just stick to the script, Joannie.

J Daniel, you seem like a really cool kid. What are you doing in a place like this?

Es Well, you see it's like this . . . I guess I have some enemies. They saw me praying to my God each day, and they convinced King Darius to pass a law saying that anyone who did that would be thrown to the lions.

J A-ha! Our catering service.

Es Be serious! No law is going to stop me from talking to my God, Mr. Lion. You see, He's my friend. King Darius is also my friend, but those wicked men tricked him and he had to stand on his promise.

J Seems to me you could've used a little better judgment when you prayed. I mean really, sitting in your window isn't exactly using your bean. *(Pause)* The script here says King, who's the King? It says a deep voice booms from up above. *(Both puppet and vent look up as deep voice speaks. Use ventriloquist voice or deep tone)*

Voice: Daniel! Daniel! I tossed and turned all night. Are you okay? Are you safe? Are you hurt?

J Oh, Brother, another reporter taking a survey!

Es King Darius, I'm A-okay! My God was with me.

Voice: Oh, Daniel! Praise be to your God! *(changes tone of voice)* And now I order Daniel's accusers to be thrown to the lions.

J   *(Pause—looking into space)*

Es   Wake up . . . you have another line.

J   Oh, dear, let's see . . . *(in bold voice)* Holy Cow . . . on your feet men . . . the catering service is back! Soup's on! *(Joannie looks at Esmerelda)* Soup's on?

Es   Yeh, my teacher said it was very creative. No one else's lion had a part.

J   I like it, Esmerelda. We'll have to do this again. Thanks. Shall we pray: Dear God,
We are so happy that we can pray to you anytime and never have to fear death. We thank you for people such as Daniel who dared to defy the king because God was so very important in his life. May we also give you an important place in our lives.   Amen.

MEMORY MEMO
(DANIEL AND THE LION)
THIS SCRIPT MAY BE READ—NO MEMORIZATION
READ OVER SO ARE FAMILIAR

WHY DOES MY TEACHER WANT TO DO ALL THAT WORK?

IDEA: *Teacher Appreciation Sunday*

Es   *(sings)* Good Morning to you, Good morning to you, Good morning dear children, Good morning to you.

J   Did you learn that in Sunday School?

Es   Yeh, and there is a second verse . . .

J   Oh, really! *(rather "here we go again" voice)*

Es   Good morning to you, Good morning to you, Good morning dear teachers, Good morning to you.

J   That's nice, Es, sounds like a good way to start the day.

Es   Joannie, have you heard the joke about the bed?

J   No.

Es   That's because it hasn't been made up yet!

69

J Esmerelda!

Es Here's one for you. How do you keep an elephant from charging?

J Es, you and your riddles. *(repeats)* How do you keep an elephant from charging? *(shrugs shoulders)*

Es Take away his credit card.

J *(frustrated)* Es, is this what you learn in Sunday School?

Es What did the man say when he lost his dog?

J Tell me.

Es Doggone!

J Okay, that's it. Tell me about your class today.

Es I like my teacher . . . she puts up with a lot . . *(pause)* . . . sometimes it's me.

J And today is a special day when we thank the teachers for all they have done.

Es Well, really, if you think about it, we kids should get a little more credit.

J What do you mean?

Es Well, the teachers get appreciated, and we're the ones who do all the work. If it wasn't for us they wouldn't be teachers.

J Esmerelda, tell me what you do to get ready for Sunday School?

Es Let's see . . . I eat my Cheerios, get dressed, get my offering and wait for you.

J Okay, tell me some of the things that you have done in your class this year.

Es It was fun! We did lots of neat stuff:
- We played review games
- We made lots of things from clay and stuff, like Bible houses and wells.
- Once we built a huge wall around a city, just like they did in the Bible times.
- We made Bible maps and put stars on our flannel charts when we learned Bible verses.
- We made puppets and wrote plays.

J Who gets all that fun stuff together and has it ready for you?

Es My teacher . . . of course . . . *(thinks a minute)* . .. I see what you mean. She works hard, doesn't she?

J She sure does, Es. It's a lot of work making class interesting and exciting.

Es Yeh. I guess every class needs a teacher . . . but WHY DOES MY TEACHER WANT TO DO ALL THAT WORK?

J *(sensitively)* You know, Esmerelda, probably one of the reasons that your teacher is teaching is because she knows how important God is in her life and she wants to share that with you.

Es So God talks to my teacher . . . she must have the 800 number.

J I guess you could say we can talk to God anytime . . . it's always toll-free, Es. God is always listening.

Es That's why my teacher says, but she also says I could learn to listen a little better.

J I'd say she has your number! Shall we pray:
Dear God,
Thank you so very much for these dedicated teachers that share their faith with us Sunday after Sunday. Because they care . . God, you just seem more real! Amen.

J *(to the children)* Can each of you say thank-you to your teachers today?

Es *(Blurts out)* THANK-YOU, MRS. . . . *(puppeteer covers puppet's mouth)* Esmerelda, just wait until you get to class!

MEMORY MEMO
(WHY DOES MY TEACHER DO ALL THAT WORK?)

SINGS: Good Morning
   -Bed
   -Elephant
   -Dog-gone
   -Rotten-Denmark

KIDS MORE CREDIT

TEACHERS APPRECIATE—WE DO WORK

DO—READY FOR SUNDAY SCHOOL
   - C—Cheerios
   - D—dressed
   - O—offering
   - W—wait

WHO GETS ALL STUFF TOGETHER?

HARD WORK—MAKE CLASS EXCITING

DO IN CLASS
   -review games
   -clay-houses, wells
   -huge wall
   -sing songs
   -stars on chart
   -make puppet
   -write plays

IMPORTANT—GOD IN HER LIFE

GOD TALKS TO TEACHER—800

GOD ALWAYS LISTENS

SADNESS

IDEA: *Sometimes a puppeteer has the opportunity to share a personal experience or loss such as this.*

Es All right, Joannie, I have some good ones this morning.

J *(Rather unenthusiastically)* Really?

Es Ok, here goes . . . What did one sailor say to the other sailor in the desert?

J I couldn't begin to know.

Es Long time no SEA . . . *(laughs—no response from Joannie—Esmerelda explains)* . . . you know S-E-A kind of sea.

J *(Still acting rather down)* Very funny.

Es OK, what is a sleeping bull called?

J *(rather irritated)* Es, I don't know!

Es A Bulldozer! *(laughs and looks at Joannie)* Boy, you sure are a barrel of fun! I think I'll save my next riddle for another Sunday.

J I just don't feel funny.

Es You can say that again. You aren't even a good sport . . . I mean sometimes you laugh even when my jokes are awful.

J I'm sorry, I guess I just feel sad today.

Es What's wrong, did you lose your last friend?

J As a matter of fact . . . yes, I did.

Es *(surprised)* You did! Well, get another one.

J *(slightly irritated)* Esmerelda, it just isn't that easy . . . *(to kids)* How many of you have a special friend? I really liked this friend.

Es Why was she so special?

J Well, Es. I guess because she was always there. One of the very lowest times in my life when my feelings were sad, my finances were at the worst and clouds were hanging over my days, she encouraged me, she took time to care.

Es Like what?

J One time when she visited me, I said "Good-bye." I walked back to my desk and there was a $50 dollar bill. I couldn't believe it. Another time she asked to borrow my car, and when she returned it, it was full of gas and four new tires, as she said I shouldn't be driving on such bald tires, it wasn't safe.

Es How Cow, she WAS a good friend!

J Es, she not only cared about my needs, but she also cared about what I felt and thought. She was like a mirror that reflected back . . . she listened and I knew she understood how I was feeling.

Es Why doesn't she stay?

J Well, she has a new dream, a new direction . . . she needs to move on.

Es Can't she find her dream here?

J The best opportunity isn't here, Es, which means she has to leave. You know, many times in life people have to leave . . . remember the day you started school . . . kids go on to college . . . or get married . . . or find new jobs . . . Jesus even left his family to preach.

Es *(in thought)* But you can't forget her because you remember so many nice things about her.

J That's true, Esmerelda.

Es And you can write her.

J I'll do that for sure.

Es But you're still sad.

J I know I need to get used to her not being around.

Es Did you tell her you were going to be this sad? Maybe she'd change her mind and stay.

J Es, I may not want her to leave, but I want her to be happy.

Es You hope she finds her dream?

J Yeh, I sure do.

Es Maybe you need to do what you tell me to do.

J What's that?

Es Talk to God . . . you tell me he's always there even when you feel all alone and sad.

J Thanks, Es, guess we all need to be reminded sometimes . . . He REALLY IS always there.

Es God cares when you are sad, Joannie, and so do I.

J *(Smiles and hugs puppet)* Thanks, Es!
Dear God,
Thank you for friends that are so special that we feel sadness when they must leave. Lord, may we be a caring and loving friend. And Lord, we know it's okay to feel sad sometimes.   Amen

MEMORY MEMO
(SADNESS)

SAILOR
SLEEPING BULL

DON'T FEEL FUNNY

LOST BEST FRIEND

WHY SO SPECIAL?
- always there
- encouraged me
- time to care
- $50
- new tires
- felt and thought

DON'T MISS CAMP!

<u>IDEA:</u> *Camp Sunday*
<u>PROPS:</u> *Puppet dressed in jeans, shorts, sweatshirt, etc. (Camp attire)*

Es *(Gutteral noises—clearing throat)*

J What's wrong with your voice?

Es I think I gotta' clear my throat. *(loud clearing sounds)*

J Esmerelda, my goodness . . . not here.

Es Is it clear? *(opens mouth very wide for Joannie to see)*

J *(Looks around)* This is very embarrassing! How am I supposed to know?

Es Ok, I'm ready . . . what do you call a pig that knows Karate?

Es A Pork Chop! Okay, what did the porcupine say to the glue?

J Got me!

Es You stick to your business, I'll stick to mine.

J Esmerelda, really!

Es What time is it when 20 dogs are chasing a cat?

J *(Disgusted tone)* What?

Es Twenty after one.

J Esmerelda, where did you learn all this stuff?

Es At camp last year.

J Oh, that is why you're wearing those jeans and sweatshirt. I didn't think you looked too "churchy" this morning.

Es Yeah, it's Camp Sunday today. We're trying to get everyone excited about going to camp. Camp is the greatest part of the summer.

J Really . . . and what all do you do?

Es We have crafts, canoeing, games, swimming, singing, nature hikes, we discuss things . . . it's just really great.

J You and I hike a lot.

Es Yeah, I figured after walking with you I should be a great hiker.

J If I was walking too fast, why didn't you tell me?

Es . . . the jet stream got in my way.

J C'mon Es.

Es You know, on the way to camp we were talking about what our moms told us before we came to camp.

J I 'spose that was interesting. Did we give good advice?

Es I guess so . . . like . . .
   - Brush your teeth before you talk to anyone
   - Remember your manners
   - Don't hog all the food at dinner

J Uh-huh, why did you write home asking me to send food?

Es Because all they serve at camp is Breakfast, Lunch, and Dinner.

J I see . . . what did some of the other moms say?

Es - Don't fall overboard
- Take a shower
- Keep dirty clothes and clean ones separate
- You told me to go to the bathroom BEFORE discussion group.

J I did? We do act too much like moms, don't we?

Es I guess that's the only way you know how to act. Discussion group was so good. We talked about how much God cares for us and that each of us could make God's world a better place.

J What a good thought, Esmerelda. Just to realize that each of us could make this world better . . . isn't that something?

Es I felt really close to God there when I saw the gorgeous lake and the sunset and the trees, when the counselor put her arm around me . . . I just know for sure there is a God.

J It is really a special experience, isn't it?

Es It is hard to describe. I made such neat friends that I sorta' cried when we had to leave. *(puppet drops head—speaks bit slower)*

J I know you talked about how you didn't want it to end.

Es I didn't! The last night we sat around the fire and sang and the feeling was so close and so great. I like to sing . . . I don't sing so good, but when lots of kids sing together, then I sound okay.

J *(chuckle)* Know what you mean. Do you remember the words of the song you sang?

Es I'll never forget it, Joannie.
(Sings)—Each campfire lights anew,
The flame of friendship true
The joy I've had in knowing you
Will last my whole life through.
(Or use any campfire song that is familiar)

J Lasting friendships are very special, Esmerelda. I hope lots of kids here can go to camp and can be as excited and thrilled about it as you. Shall we pray:
Dear God,

Thank you so much for the joy and fun of camp. Thank you for all those that make it possible . . . and especially, thank you for a chance to know you better, God.
Amen.

(On leaving:)

Es Joannie, they have camps for old people like you too, you know!

J OLD! Esmerelda, really.

MEMORY MEMO
(DON'T MISS CAMP)

VOICE
PIG—KARATE?
PORCUPINE—GLUE
20 DOGS CHASE CAT

CAMP SUNDAY DO:
- crafts
- canoeing
- games
- swimming
- singing
- nature hikes
- discussion

MOM'S ADVICE
- Brush teeth
- Manners
- Don't hog food

BREAKFAST, LUNCH, DINNER
OTHER MOMS SAY:
- overboard
- shower
- dirty—clean—separate
- bathroom

TALKED ABOUT GOD—WORLD BETTER

CLOSE TO GOD
- gorgeous lake-sunset-trees
- counselor
- didn't want to end
- feeling close

SINGS

HOPE LOTS OF KIDS GO TO CAMP!

STAY OUT OF THE POTATO CHIPS

IDEA: *Father's Day (Father's demands on Esmerelda misinterpreted)*

J Good Morning, Esmerelda!

Es What's good about it?

J It's a great day. The sun is shining and we are all here in church.

Es I'd like to sleep! That's my idea of a good time. *(Closes eyes and begins to snore)*

J Esmerelda, just because you stayed up late last night . . . don't take it out on us. See all these shining faces on the boys and girls.

Es What happened to _____ and _____ *(names of ministers or teachers in the congregation that kids would know)*. Did they sleep in today?

J Of course not. Just what is the matter with you today?

Es I'm tired and hungry.

J I know what would make you feel better.

Es Me too . . . a huge Hardee Burger with onion, lettuce, cheese, tomato, and bacon with fries and a shake!

J Esmerelda! When you get in this awful mood, you need someone to talk to. Do you feel like talking?

Es *(Disgusted tone)* Not really. I had a stupid week.

J And just what does a stupid week consist of?

Es I goofed up on my math test. I had to sit by the teacher on the bus, on our field trip, so I didn't dare chew the gum I had in my pocket. On Wednesday I went in the wrong restroom and Friday I tripped on my shoelaces and my books slid right over the principal's feet and my gum got stuck in my hair!

J Wow! Is there anything else that went wrong?

Es Yeah, I saved the worst for last. I think I'm gonna' run away from home. My dad hates me!

J Just a minute here, Esmerelda. What would ever make you think that?

Es He's always on me for something. I can't seem to do anything right. He says, "Don't watch too much T.V." or "Tidy up your room," or "Stay out of the Potato Chips" and "Practice the piano." I've had enough!

J Esmerelda, let's talk about this. Why do you think he wants you to do those things?

Es He just hates me, that's why.

J I really think you have the wrong idea . . . why do you think your dad doesn't want you to watch so much TV?

Es He says some is okay, but he says he'd rather have me read a book 'cuz it puts better thoughts in my head.

J That sounds logical. Why do you think he wants you to keep things tidy?

Es Well, he said he didn't want our house to look like the city dump! He says Mom works hard and we should help out.

J That also sounds pretty reasonable to me.

Es That's 'cuz you're an adult.

J I know you like baseball and sports, Esmerelda.

Es What's that got to do with anything?

J Well, that idea of your dad's, "not so many potato chips" and more fruits and vegetables is sensible.

Es I don't get it.

J Well, if you don't eat well, you won't have a healthy body so you can do well in sports. Seems to me that your dad cares a lot about you.

Es Holy Cow, I never thought of it that way. But Joannie, this is the last straw . . . I asked my dad if my friend, Lou, could stay overnight, and he said it would be okay . . . but then he changed his mind and said she couldn't come at all!

J Okay, Esmerelda. Let's back up. Tell me what really happened.

Es *(slowly)* Well . . . Dad said if I got my practicing done, my chores finished, and my math completed by 6 p.m. that Lou could come over.

J Did you get it done?

Es Nope. But I thought as long as I had already asked Lou he wouldn't make me call her back and say that she couldn't come, but he did! I was TREMENDOUSLY UPSET!

J Es, who's to blame?

Es *(hanging head—speak slowly)* I guess it really was my fault. Dad made a deal with me and I didn't keep my end of the bargain.

J You know something, Es, I think you have a very special dad who really cares about you.

Es Well . . . I guess you're right. I guess I shouldn't have doubted my dad's love. I guess he just wants me to be a good kid, huh?

J You bet he does! Shall we pray:
Dear God,
Thank you for Fathers that care enough to teach us and guide us. But most of all we thank you for fathers that show us Your love that we might also become Your child. Amen.

79

MEMORY MEMO
(STAY OUT OF THE POTATO CHIPS!)

WHAT'S GOOD ABOUT IT?
- up late
- what's matter with you?
- tired—hungry
- Hardee burger

STUPID WEEK
- goofed—math
- sit teacher—bus
- couldn't chew gum
- wrong restroom
- tripped
- books—principal's feet
- gum—hair

DAD HATES ME
- Nothing right
- too much TV
- stay out of potato chips
- practice piano

WHY DAD WANTS THIS:
- cares a lot about you
- never thought of it that way
- Lou could stay over
- practice, chores, math by 6 p.m.
- tremendously upset

WHO'S TO BLAME?
- didn't keep bargain
- a dad that really cares

SHOULDN'T HAVE DOUBTED HIS LOVE

CHANGES

<u>IDEA:</u> Changes that happen in our lives

J   Hey, Es, Good Morning! What a beautiful warm sunny day!

Es   Joannie, it's downright hot!

J   You do look a bit warm.

Es   Whew, but guess what my friend Lou and I did this week? We had a lemonade stand.

J   That's great. I know you just finished school. Is it okay if I test your math?

Es   Ah . . . I guess so.

J   Okay . . . If I have 10 glasses of lemonade and drank nine, what would I have?

Es   A belly-ache.

J   No. I mean, how may glasses would I have left?

Es Oh, you mean if I had 10 glasses of lemonade and you drank nine, how many would I have left?

J Yes.

Es None.

J What?

Es I DRANK THE OTHER GLASS!

J Why did you do that?

Es I was thirsty!

J So much for Math. Did you like literature?

Es It's okay. We were going to talk about the nursery rhymes at the end of the year, just for fun . . . *(sadly)* but we didn't have time. Our teacher says kids today don't have much appreciation for those.

J That's for sure . . . why I knew all those by heart . . . Old Woman in a Shoe . . . Jack Sprat . . . Simple Simon . . . Little Miss Muffet . . . and many more.

Es Say one for me.

J OK, how about Miss Muffet?

Es Okay, shoot!

J Little Miss Muffet sat on a tuffet . . .

Es What's a tuffet?

J Well, I don't really know. Probably some sort of hassock.

Es What's a hassock?

J I guess you'd say some sort of stool.

Es Like my TV stool?

J Yes, like your TV stool. Anyway . . .

Es That's a dumb name. I never heard of anyone with the name Muffet.

J It's probably a made-up name to rhyme with tuffet. Poets do things like that.

Es Why?

J Look, do you want to hear the rest of it or not?

Es Yes.

J Little Miss Muffet sat on a tuffet / Eating her curds and whey . . .

Es What's curds and whey?

J It's stuff you get when you make cheese. The curds float around in the whey.

Es Yuck! It sounds terrible!

J *(to audience)* How come I didn't ask these questions when I was her age and somebody read this stuff to me. OK, so you wouldn't eat it. Miss Muffet loved it! Let's go on. I think the rest of it goes something like this: A great big spider sat down beside her and frightened Miss Muffet away.

Es Not me! I'm not scared of spiders.

J Look, Es, you started me thinking. I don't think that is a very good nursery rhyme. Not for today's kids anyway. It needs to be revised or brought up to date.

Es Can I do it?

J Sure . . . go ahead, if you think you can improve on the great mind that wrote it.

Es *(thinking . . . hums a bit . . . talks to self under breath)*

J C'mon Es.

Es Ok . . . ok . . . how about this: Little Miss Rosy O'Toole / Sat on her TV stool / Stashing her dinner away / When a great big spider / Sat down beside her / She bashed out its brains with a tray!

J Well . . . that's up to date all right! You know, Esmerelda, I was thinking . . . what I accepted and appreciated as a child has changed. Some nursery rhymes seem silly to you and need to be changed. But it got me to thinking about other changes in our lives.

Es How do you mean?

J Not small changes like nursery rhymes, but big changes.

Es You mean like getting out of school?

J   No, that's a nice change. Some changes are hard, like losing a good friend, or moving to a new school, graduation, getting married, or a new job.

Es   My friend, Veronica, her mom and dad got a divorce. Everyone is really sad.

J   It's so hard when you hurt inside.

Es   My friend, Ellie, her grandma had a stroke and she can't talk. Ellie is so scared for her gramma.

J   *(Gently)* Wow, what a change for her—or a doctor says it's cancer . . . it changes your whole life.

Es   I don't think I like big changes. They hurt too much. It's scary!

J   Es, there is one thing that doesn't change . . . God's love for us.

Es   It's like having your best friend beside you.

J   Please believe that, Es. He's not only a friend, but He cares and understands.

Es   I guess lots of things are gonna change, aren't they, Joannie?

J   You are right, but God's love for us, it just never changes.

Es   Never?

J   That's right.

Es   Wow, it's nice there is one thing that never changes!

J   *(Gives puppet a hug)* Shall we pray:

Dear God,
Thank you for this time together. Thank you for changes that make us grow and make us know when others hurt. May we reach out, be their friend, care, and let them know of your love.
Amen.

MEMORY MEMO
(CHANGES)

LEMONADE STAND

TEST MATH—10 glasses lemonade
  —drank 9

LITERATURE—nursery rhymes
  - Little Miss Muffet
    - tuffet—hassock—stool
    - dumb name—Muffet (rhyme)
    - curds—whey
      - make cheese
      - terrible

*HOW COME—NEVER ASKED THESE
QUESTIONS?*

*NURSERY RHYMES NOT VERY GOOD
FOR TODAY*

REVISED POEM—ESMERELDA

OTHER CHANGES—LIFE CHANGES
    - Losing friend
    - new school
    - graduation
    - married
    - new job
    - divorce
    - gramma—stroke

DON'T LIKE BIG CHANGES

GOD DOESN'T CHANGE

STARS AND STRIPES

<u>IDEA:</u> *4th of July*
<u>PROP:</u> *Flag—colors: Purple circles for stars—orange and green stripes (only 7 stripes)*
Dollar bill

Es Hey, Joannie, on a baseball team, which player makes the best pancakes?

J You got me!

Es The batter.

J Why can't I ever get those?

Es Okay, what do you call a vacuum race?

J I'm not even going to try that one.

Es A Kirby Derby!

J I'm going to change the subject . . . what are you doing?

Es I'm re-doing the American Flag.

J What for?

Es Some of us kids are going to be in the 4th of July Parade, and I'm making the flag.

J But why are you using green, orange and purple?

Es Well, I thought I'd use some different colors seeing as we have been using the same colors for over 200 years. It's time for a change.

J *(Joannie looking at flag)* What are these purple things up here in the corner?

Es They are purple circles.

Es I thought I'd put circles instead of stars. They are a lot easier to make, you know.

J And how come you only have 7 stripes?

Es I got tired of making them. Anyway thirteen is unlucky.

J Esmerelda, do you know what those thirteen stripes stand for?

Es Nope.

J   The thirteen stripes stand for the 13 original colonies of our country.

Es   Really?

J   And the stars, Es, they stand for each state in America. There should be 50.

Es   Oh, oh, guess I'm a little short.

J   And one other thing, do you know why the flag is red, white and blue?

Es   I guess I don't.

J   The red stands for the blood that was shed to make the United States a free country, the blue stands for loyalty and the white for purity.

Es   I didn't know that. That's pretty neat.

J   You see, Es, it isn't just a flag, it's a reminder of what this country has stood for for over 200 years.

Es   I guess we really shouldn't change it, should we?

J   We should be proud of it!

Es   You know, come to think of it, purple, orange and green don't quite cut it.

J   I guess I like it the way Betsy Ross designed it.

Es   My teacher says we are really lucky to live in America.

J   Es, she is certainly right. We have a beautiful country, we can vote as we please, we can go to the church of our choice, freedom to travel anywhere.

Es   We have good schools, lots of food to eat . . .

J   You even have the opportunity to become a millionaire!

Es   Only in America . . .

J   Many countries in the world are not that lucky.

Es   It's not all good, Joannie. People kill each other, they steal, some are dishonest.

J   That's where each one of us comes in. We can help this country become even greater.

Es   How?

J The first leaders of our country had a dream to make this country great. They wanted "one nation under God."

Es Maybe that's the part we forget sometimes.

J You are so right Es. Look what I have here! *(holds up a dollar)* Can you read what it says here? *(holds dollar for her to read)*

Es It says, *(reads slowly)* "In God we trust." Wow!

J That's what our country was founded on, trust in God.

Es That's cool. I'll have to show my friends.

J And especially on July 4th we need to think about why our country was founded.

Es First I have to make a new flag for the parade.

J *(Joannie looks at Es)*

Es It will be red, white and blue, and 50 stars!

J I like that! Happy 4th of July everyone!

Es Joannie, can I say the prayer today?

J Sure.

Es Dear God,
Thank you so much for this wonderful country where we are free to come to church today. Our great, great grandfathers were right when they said, "In God we trust." Thank you for this day to remember. Amen.

MEMORY MEMO
(STARS AND STRIPES)

JOKES
    Baseball team—Pancakes—Batter
    Vacuum Race—Kirby Derby

RE-DOING FLAG
    GREEN, ORANGE, PURPLE
    Circles for Stars—easier make
    Seven stripes—13 unlucky

STAND FOR:
    13 colonies
    50 states
    Red—blood shed
    Blue—loyalty
    White—purity

REMINDER OF WHAT COUNTRY STANDS FOR
    Shouldn't change it
    Be proud of it

FREEDOMS
    Vote
    Church of choice
    Travel
    Schools
    Food to eat
    Millionaire

ONE NATION UNDER GOD

DOLLAR BILL—"In God We Trust"

EIGHT WEEKS FOR DELIVERY!

IDEA: *Jealousy*
PROPS: *Use of two puppets*
Fancy hair clip
Form (pinned to puppet hand)

Es Joannie, guess what? I did it! I did it!

J Did what?

Es I ate four boxes of cereal and now I have enough proof of purchase seals.

J Enough for what?

Es To send for my "highfalutin'-hip-happiness hat."

J A highfalutin'-hip-happiness hat?

Es Yeh, see here. *(shows form)* I can't wait to get it. It will be so cool!

J *(looks at form)* Lots of neat colors, red, green, blue and yellow. *(Pause, reads form)* It says here to allow eight to ten weeks for delivery.

Es *(loud, irritated voice)* EIGHT TO TEN WEEKS! I'll be old then!

J Well, Esmerelda, I'm sure that your happiness hat will be the talk of the college campus.

Es That isn't fair. My friend Lou, her dad gave her this real neat _____ *(local team or NFL Team)* hat. Everyone thinks it's real cool.

J I get it. So you thought if you sent for this cereal offer everyone would notice yours.

Es Well . . . maybe.

J Do you 'spose if you got a hat that it would take away from Lou's . . . that she would feel badly?

Es Naw! A little competition is good for everyone, right?

J While we're thinking about that, I really want you to meet someone, Esmerelda.

(At this point, puppeteer reaches down and slips into another puppet—Alvia or this could be a child)

J Esmerelda, I would like to have you meet Alvia Morgistad.

A Hi, Esmerelda.

Es Alvia . . . that sure is a dumb name . . . Alvia Morgistad . . . Holy Cow, and some people think Esmerelda is awful!

J Es, I am really embarrassed.

Es Well, her name sounds like a pain killer . . . an aspirin.

J What?

Es It does . . . you know . . .

J No, Esmerelda . . . it's not Advil, her name is Alvia.

Es It's still weird!

A Does she always act this way?

J Esmerelda, Alvia's mother is very sick in the hospital, so she came to live with her aunt for awhile, so I thought it would be nice if she could meet everyone here.

Es Joannie, did you read the bulletin?

J What do you mean?

Es Well, under Children's Sermon, it says Esmerelda and Joannie, it doesn't say anything about Advil.

J It's Alvia.

Es Well, it doesn't say anything about her either.

J Es, are you jealous?

Es Jealous? Me? Naw!

J You haven't even said, "Hello."

Es (rather half-heartedly) Hello, Alvia.

J You know, Es, Alvia has a rather interesting hobby.

Es She probably collects some useless thing . . .

J You mean like cereal proof of purchase seals? Alvia, tell Esmerelda what you do.

A Well, Esmerelda, my gramma taught me to make these hair ornaments, *(she turns her head—is wearing one—Esmerelda examines the hair ornament)* See, they are made of material, buttons, ribbon and lace.

Es *(excited)* Wow! Those are super-colossal. No one here in _____ *(name of church or town)* has one like that. That is neater than a happiness hat!

A I could make you one. You just have to tell me what colors you like.

Es Well, it has to go with green. *(color of puppet used)*

A That's no problem. If you just want to stop over after church we'll get started and . . .

J Say, before you two get carried away with your plans here, can I say something?

Es I don't know if I want to hear it.

J Esmerelda, you didn't seem very concerned about getting a hat that would make Lou's _____ *(team name)* hat seem rather common compared to the one you wanted to order, yet you felt very badly when I invited Alvia today, because you felt she might draw attention away from you.

Es I just wanted to be cool . . . I WAS jealous . . . I wanted a hat like Lou's . . . Alvia has pretty hair and clothes . . . maybe I thought you'd like her better.

J You almost missed making a friend . . . you can be so jealous that you don't really get to know someone. And you know what else . . . you were downright rude!

Es I know I was. I'm sorry, Alvia.

A That's okay.

J Remember this, Esmerelda: It's nice to be important, but it's more important to be nice.

Es Alvia . . . you'll see, she always get the last word.

A *(repeats)* It's nice to be important, but it's more important to be nice. That is good, Esmerelda. I want to remember that. *(possibly kids could repeat after the puppet)*

J Shall we pray:
Dear God,
Help us not to be jealous of others. God has made us each special with something to share. Thank you for friends that care. Amen.

MEMORY MEMO
(EIGHT WEEKS FOR DELIVERY)

PROOF OF PURCHASE SEALS
   —highfalutin-hip-happiness-hat
EIGHT-TEN WEEKS—DELIVERY
   - Lou's hat
   - Competition
ALVIA
   - Dumb name
   - Pain killer
   - Mother sick
   - Hobby

HAIR ORNAMENTS
   - Super-colossal
   - help make one
JEALOUS
   - Missed making a friend
   - Rude
It's nice to be important, but more important to be nice!
PRAYER

GOIN' FISHIN'
SCRIPTURE—MARK 1:16-22

IDEA: *Fishers of Men*
PROP: *Fishing Pole, help by puppet.*
Tackle box (where can be reached) and can with Worms written on it

J Good Morning, kids. Hi, Esmerelda . . . Hey, it looks like you're going fishing.

Es Yep, right after church *(or Sunday School)* . . . that's what I'm gonna' do . . . ya know when I get big . . . I'm gonna' be a fisherwoman and get rich.

J Es, do you really think you can get rich being a fisherwoman?

Es Sure! All their business is NET profit!

J *(Rolls eyes)* Do you like fishing as much as baseball?

Es *(Pause)* Well . . . that's hard, but my dad sure does.

J He does?

Es My definition of a guy who loves to fish is . . . a FINatic!

J Esmerelda!

Es My dad says he loves to fish, 'cuz he can sit on a riverbank and do nothing . . . but at home mom won't let him get away with it!

91

J Hummmmmm, is that right. You just may've enlightened a few moms here today. I see you have your tackle box here so you're all equipped for the day.

Es Sure am.

J Can I look inside?

Es Sure.

J *(opens tackle box—sorts thru contents)* Esmerelda! What on earth . . . ? M&M's, licorice, gummy bears, tootsie rolls . . .

Es Well, dad brings all the hooks and stuff. I bring the important stuff.

J Well, you certainly aren't going to get hungry . . . did your mom see all this stuff?

Es Shhhhhhhh . . . she doesn't know everything. She'd probably put in carrot sticks and apples . . . so I packed it myself!

J Ya know, Es, speaking of water, fishing, etc., I wonder if Noah spent a lot of time fishing when he was on the ark.

Es Joannie! *(emphatically)* I DON'T think so . . . remember he only had two worms!

J Speaking about the Bible, they did lots of fishing in Bible times.

Es I know just last Sunday our Sunday School teacher talked about being fishers of men.

J She did?

Es I wonder what kind of bait I should use? Dad has a red and white thing . . . and he also has a green thing with big eyes . . . maybe that would work.

J Esmerelda, do you know what your teacher meant when she was talking about being fishers of men?

Es Well, if those lures won't work maybe a net . . . a big one!

J You see, Es, some of Jesus' disciples were fishermen before Jesus asked them to follow him.

Es They fished back then?

J They sure did. Peter, Andrew, James and John all fished for a living. It was their job.

Es They fished for fish, right?

J Of course.

Es Then what's all this "fishers of men" stuff?

J When Jesus called these men to be his disciples they left their job *(fishing)* and their families to be with Jesus.

Es Really?

J And Jesus said, "I will make you fishers of men."

Es I wonder what kind of bait they used?

J No, Es, they didn't use bait.

Es Well, what did they use?

J Let me see if I can explain this to you . . . You see, when Jesus asked the disciples to follow him, he wanted to teach them about God and his love, so they could share it with other people. Many people heard about Jesus and God's love from the disciples, and they believed.

Es I get it . . . they were CAUGHT by God's love.

J I guess you could say that.

Es Ya know what, Joannie, I'm smarter than I thought.

J And how's that?

Es My tackle box . . .

J Yeh.

Es What I have in it . . . is much better for catching men than fish.

J You are certainly right there, Esmerelda! Shall we pray:
Dear God,
Thank you that we too can be fishers of men by sharing God's love with others. That we can bring our friends to Sunday School where they learn about you.
Amen.

MEMORY MEMO
(GOIN' FISHIN')

GOIN' FISHIN'
    Rich Fisherwoman
    Net Profit

GUY WHO LOVES TO FISH—FINatic

TACKLE BOX
    M&M'S, Licorice, Gummy, Tootsie

NOAH—two worms

FISHING—Bible Times

FISHING—Bible Times
    Fishers of Men
    Bait
    Big Net
    Jesus' Disciples were fishermen
    Left families to be with Jesus
    Jesus wanted to teach about God's love

CAUGHT BY GOD'S LOVE
    Tackle box—better for catching men

PRAYER

EVERYONE IS SPECIAL TO GOD
EPHESIANS 1:3-14

PROPS: *Rabbit Ears*

Es What do you think of that sign on the church bulletin board?

J What did it say?

Es Come early if you want a back seat.

J Well, that is a different twist.

Es Yeh, speaking of doing things differently, I guess last Sunday
_____*(gives last name of Pastor)*.

J *(interrupts)* Es, it's Rev. _____ *(pastor's name)*

Es Well, REV. _____ *(gives Pastor's full name)* fouled up the routine.

J He did?

Es Yeah, he didn't stand at the door and shake hands with the worshipers
after the service.

J What did he do?

Es He went out to the curb and shook hands with the red-faced parents
waiting for their kids to come out of Sunday School.

94

J   *(hand over mouth)* He did. Rather ingenious.

Es   That's 'cuz you weren't one of them!

J   Could be, Esmerelda.

Es   Joannie, I have a question. Why do they say AMEN in church instead of AWOMAN?

J   Why do they say Amen instead of Awoman? *(thinks a minute)* Because we sing HYMNS not HERS, I guess.

Es   Holy Cow, Joannie, ask an intelligent question and get a silly answer!
(Beings to sing)
Jesus loves the little children,
All the children of the world,
Green, green, green and green, they are precious in his sight.
Jesus loves the green children of the world.
(Or use whatever color or characteristic of your puppet)

J   All right, Esmerelda. You know that isn't right! God loves all the children of the world, not just green ones.

Es   I was just singing the song my way. You know, Joannie, we always sing the song Red, Brown, Yellow, Black and White, but they never include my color, green.

J   But Es, that's only a song. Just because it doesn't include green, it doesn't mean that God doesn't love you. They couldn't possibly put every color in a song. God loves everybody.

Es   I guess I know that.

J   What are you wearing today?

Es   EARS . . . SEE! When I grow up, I want to be Bugs Bunny.

J   Esmerelda, you can't be Bugs Bunny! He's a guy and you're a girl. Anyway, he's not even real!

Es   Okay, then I'll be the Little Mermaid.

J   She's not real either.

Es   How about Power Rangers?

J   Nope, sorry. *(Esmerelda hangs head)* What's wrong?

Es I know, I'll be Aladdin on the flying carpet.

J Esmerelda, what's wrong with being yourself?

Es Well, Bugs Bunny is so real! Little Mermaid, Power Rangers and Aladdin too, I saw them on television. So there!

J Es! Honestly! Those are just actors playing roles.

Es Oh yeah, well then, just how did they make an actor fly if he wasn't Aladdin? Huh?

J It's special effects, tricks with the camera.

Es Are you sure?

J Uh-huh. But that doesn't matter. Why don't you just want to be you?

Es I'm not anyone special. I'm not important.

J Esmerelda, I'd like to tell you a story.

Es Great! I love stories.

J This is a story about a king who walked into his garden and everything was withering and dying.

Es Why?

J Well, the king talked to an oak tree near the gate, and he learned that it was sick of life because it was not tall and beautiful like the pine. The pine was upset, for it could not bear delicious fruit like the apple tree, when the apple tree complained that it did not have the lovely smell of the spruce; and so it went throughout the garden.

Es No one liked who they were?

J That's right, Es. Coming to a pansy, however, the king saw its bright face full of cheerfulness.
"Well, little flower," said the king, "I'm glad to find at least one that is happy in this awful wilting garden."
"Your majesty, I know I'm very small, but I decided that you wanted a pansy when you planted me. If you had wanted an oak or apple tree, you would have put one in my place. So I decided to be the best little flower I can be!"

Es Wow! I guess we ARE all special. It sure would be boring if we all were like everyone else. Imagine if everyone in this church was a Ventriloquist!

J That would be something! But Es, you and all these kids are God's children, and he loves you dearly.

Es How do I know he loves me?

J He loved all of us so much, that's why he sent his son Jesus to show us what his love was all about.

Es If God cared enough to do that, I guess I must be pretty important after all.

J Of course you are!

Es But I still have one question.

J Oh, what's that?

Es How do I love him back? What can I give to God?

J You can give something to God that only you can give.

Es What?

J You can give God the love in your heart. When you give God that love, it just spills over onto everyone around you. It can change the world.

Es Holy Cow, isn't that great!

J Shall we pray:
Dear God,
We know how important each one of us is to you, for it is through us you spread your word of love. Help us to be more loving. Amen.

Es *(as leaving)* Guess I can throw these ears away seeing as I'm gonna' just be me!

MEMORY MEMO
(EVERYONE IS SPECIAL TO GOD)

CHURCH BULLETIN BOARD
PASTOR—curb—shook hands
AMEN—AWOMAN
HYMNS NOT HERS
SING: Jesus loves little children
    - Green-green-green *(color of puppet)*
    - only song—God loves everybody
EARS—Bugs Bunny
    - Little Mermaid
    - Power Rangers
    - Aladdin
WHY NOT BE YOURSELF
    - not special
    - not important

STORY
    - King—garden—dying
    - Oak tree—sick life—not tall like pine
    - Pine tree—upset—couldn't bear fruit—apple
    - Apple—complained—lovely smell—spruce
    - Pansy
    - cheerful
    - very small—decided you wanted me
    - best flower I can be

BORING IF EVERYONE WAS ALIKE

97

EVERYONE GOD'S CHILDREN—HE LOVES EVERYONE
- Send Son
- how love God back
- Give Him love in our heart
- Spills over to everyone around
- Change the world

August

THE SEQUOIA TREE

IDEA: *Vacation*
PROP: *Could use picture of Sequoia tree if available*

Es Did you miss me, Joannie?

J I certainly did. When you are gone it is far too quiet.

Es I GUESS we had a pretty good vacation.

J You GUESS?

Es Well, dad thought if we camped we could save some money, but it didn't turn out so good.

J What happened?

Es We headed west, and we set this tent up by a pretty lake.

J Sounds nice.

Es Well, my front teeth had been real loose. I ran into my brother and knocked one out, and mom wiggled the other tooth and it came out, so I put my teeth under my pillow in the tent.

J Guess you didn't eat any corn on the cob on this vacation.

Es That's for sure . . . well, that night it started to rain. It got real cloudy. Mom and Dad went to the car and listened to the weather report.

J What was it?

Es It was a tornado watch, so my parents took us kids into the ladies bathroom . . . it was so windy and raining, the bathroom leaked.

J Did you spend the night there?

Es I think so . . . finally dad went out and our tent had blown away. I was `really upset because my teeth were in there!

J Oh, that's right.

Es And you know what was worse?

J What?

Es I had asked the tooth fairy for a raise!

J So what happened?

Es My little brother slept through this whole thing! But can you believe it, Dad rescued my teeth!

J That SURE was lucky.

Es I was very happy! When the wind stopped I asked Mom if I could go out and play in the rain.

J I 'spose she didn't like that idea.

Es Not only that, she said I'd get soaked, maybe catch pneumonia, have to go to the hospital, run up a terrible bill and miss our vacation.

J Wow, that would be awful!

Es Sometimes when you ask mom you get the worst . . . I never dreamed a little rain could be so dangerous.

J She cares about you, Es.

Es Well, after all this Dad says "let's pack up and go out for breakfast."

J Sounds like a good idea.

Es We went into this little place. I guess the cereal was okay, but there was this old man and he was using terrible language.

J He was swearing?

Es Yeh, ya know Mom doesn't use any bad words, but she sure knows one when she hears one!

J Did you finally get everything dried out?

Es We did! Everybody at the campground "helped each other." Another man even helped my dad sew a tear in our tent.

J   How nice!

Es   Well, finally we headed out to California, and guess what we saw?

J   Es, California is a big place.

Es   Well, we took this tour of these giant trees.

J   Giant trees?

Es   Yeh, they are called sequoias.

J   I've heard of them. They are absolutely huge.

Es   They are tremendously huge. I've never seen such trees! And the guide pointed out that the sequoia tree has roots that just barely go under the ground.

J   You mean the trees are that big, but don't have much root?

Es   Dad couldn't believe it. He grew up on a farm and he said, if the roots don't go deep, a strong wind will blow the tree over.

J   So what did the guide say?

Es   He said, "not sequoia trees. They grow only in groves and their roots intertwine together under the earth, so when strong winds come they hold each other up."

J   That's really neat . . . you know, there's a real lesson here.

Es   A lesson?

J   Yeh, Es, people are like those giant sequoias. Our families, our friends, neighbors, the church . . . they are a refuge, so when the strong winds of life blow, these people can work together to hold each other up.

Es   Strong winds of life?

J   By that, Es, I mean when bad things happened . . .

Es   You mean like getting sick, or losing a job, or having someone die?

J   Yes, but even in your campground, the people that helped you were like those sequoia trees.

Es   They were. Mom said they were a blessing. I'd like to be like a sequoia tree.

J   Es, you can be. *(to congregation)* We all can be . . . shall we pray:

Dear God:
May we as a church be like the giant sequoia trees, holding each other up in times of trouble. May we support our friends and our family the way you have always been there for us. Amen.

MEMORY MEMO
(THE SEQUOIA TREE)

VACATION
- Tooth
- Weather
- Tent blew over
- Teeth in tent

PLAY IN RAIN
- Soaked
- catch pneumonia
- hospital
- run up bill
- miss vacation

BREAKFAST
- Swearing
- mom

EVERYONE HELPED EACH OTHER

HUGE TREE
- Roots barely under ground
- Grow only in groves
- Wind—hold each other up

PEOPLE—CAMPGROUND—LIKE SEQUOIA TREES
- Blessing
- Congregation

PRAYER

NEVER AGAIN!

IDEA: *Never say Never—deals with anger*
PROPS: *Telephone*

J   Good Morning, Esmerelda! Isn't it a wonderful, beautiful, great day!

Es   *(rather short and little feeling)* What's good about it?

J   It's hard to believe that summer is almost over and school will begin soon.

Es   I'm certainly not ready for that!

J   Did you play softball this week?

Es   Yeh, and I struck out twice!

J   *(Es in down mood—Joannie tries to be up)* Humm, better luck next time. How about swimming? Have you been to the pool?

Es   They have all these stupid rules at the pool. You can't run, you can't snap your towel . . really dumb.

J   Well, you certainly are in an awful mood this morning.

Es I like it that way.

J   You do?

Es Don't even try to cheer me up.

J   Would you like to talk about it?

Es Not really.

J   Es, I'm starting to wonder why we came up here today. I wish you'd talk to me.

Es *(Half-heartedly)* Okay, what do you want to hear?

J   I guess I'd like to know what is bothering you.

Es Okay, I'll tell you . . . you know my friend Lou?

J   Of course.

Es Well, I was at her house and she got this really neat Barbie house and she has all the neat clothes and furniture.

J   Sounds really fun to me.

Es Well, she wanted to be Barbie and I was 'spose to be Ken.

J   Yeh.

Es *(raises voice)* Well, I DIDN'T want to be Ken.

J   I see.

Es I wanted to be Barbie.

J   So what happened?

Es Well, I threw Ken on the floor and his arm came off. Lou got really mad and I left.

J   . . . no wonder you are feeling awful.

Es Last Sunday in class our teacher said we should invite other kids to class so I asked Lou to come . . .

J   Is she going to come?

Es Well, when I left I said I was never coming to her house again, and she said she was never coming to Sunday School because last time she came they didn't give her a nametag.

J A nametag?

Es Yeh, see last time in Sunday School everyone got a dog or cat nametag . . . I told Lou that was really dumb, the teacher just forgot.

J I'm sure she did, Es. That's too bad all this happened. Can I ask you a question?

J You said you're never going to Lou's house again?

Es That's right!

J Okay, let's say you go to a restaurant and get some bad food and you get sick.

Es Yeh?

J Would you stop eating for the rest of your life?

Es Holy Cow, no! Gotta have my burger and fries!

J Okay, suppose you were given a counterfeit $10 dollar bill . . .

Es Counterfeit?

J Es, that means it's not real . . . would you quit using money?

Es Of course not!

J Well, just because you didn't want to be Ken, does that mean you'll never go to Lou's house? Or just because Lou didn't get a nametag, does that mean she won't go back to Sunday School?

Es I guess it doesn't make much sense, does it? But Lou, she doesn't understand who God is. She says she can't see him, or hear him, or touch him . . . so why believe. I didn't know what to say.

J God isn't hiding from us, Es. You know that is why he sent Jesus so we could better understand who he is. If we know Jesus better we will understand God, his love and caring for each of us.

Es I like coming to Sunday School to learn about Jesus. *(hangs head)* I guess I didn't act very much like him at Lou's, did I?

(TELEPHONE RINGS)

J   Hello, yes she is . . . Es, it's for you.

Es   For me?

J   Yes.

Es   Hello . . . oh . . . Hi Lou . . . yeah . . . yeah . . . okay . . . yeah.

J   Make it short.

Es   Yeah, I'm sorry too . . . tomorrow . . . sure. That's great. I'll tell my teacher. Bye, Lou.

J   It sounds like things worked out.

Es   Yep, I guess we SHOULDN'T ever say NEVER.

J   Would you like to pray:

Es   Sure.
Dear God,
Thank you for showing yourself to us in Jesus. Help me not to get so angry when things don't go my way. Thank you for friends who can say they are sorry.   Amen.

MEMORY MEMO
(NEVER AGAIN)

GOOD MORNING—"What's good about it"
- Softball
- Swimming
- Awful mood

TALK TO ME—bothering you
- Barbie—didn't want to be Ken
- Arm came off
- Invited to Sunday School
- Didn't get nametag

QUESTIONS:
- Restaurant—bad food—stop eating?
- $10 bill—counterfeit—quit using money?

LOU DOESN'T UNDERSTAND GOD—
Can't:
- see
- hear
- touch
- so why believe

*LIKE SUNDAY SCHOOL—
LEARN ABOUT JESUS*

TELEPHONE
Worked things out
"I guess we
shouldn't ever say never"

DEPENDABILITY IS A BIG WORD

IDEA: *God's world is dependable—we should also be dependable*

Es Hey, kids, why was Cinderella kicked off the baseball team?

J Es, do we have to start this way?

Es C'mon, Joannie, be a sport.

J Why was Cinderella kicked off the baseball team? Okay, let's have it.

Es She ran away from the ball.

J *(Groans)*

Es What did the octopus say to the other octopus?

J *(bit irritated)* What?

Es I want to shake your hand, your hand, your hand, your hand, your hand . . .

J Okay, okay, we got it! You know what I think?

Es What?

J You are just avoiding talking to me about yesterday.

Es Oh, *(slowly)* you mean when you asked me to clean my room.

J That's exactly what I mean.

Es Well . . . you see, it's real hard to put everything in it's place when most of my stuff doesn't have a place.

J That's just it. I think I have offered more incentives to pick up clothes than the airlines have offered people to fly.

Es Well, that list on my closet door was real cute, Joannie.

J What?

Es You know that one that said:
#1. Locate closet
#2. Grasp triangle-shaped metal object called a hanger
#3. Hold hanger while reaching down, picking up shirt you are standing on.
#4. Insert clothes on hanger and see that it is neat.

#5. Locate pole in closet—normal position of pole is horizontal.
#6. Hang clothes on pole—if shirt falls to floor, repeat steps 4, 5, and 6.

J   Guess I'm going to have to try a different incentive. I was really disappointed you didn't do your part, Es. I was having company and I was counting on you to clean your room. Dependability is really important!

Es Dependability is a very big word!

J   Es, it means I can count on you. You will do what you say.

Es Sure be nice if we didn't have to be so "Dependable."

J   Would it? Let me ask you a question. What if the world stopped turning and we had winter all year?

Es Holy Cow, Joannie, no swimming, or boating, or lying in the sun.

J   Or it could be summer all year . . .

Es All moms would certainly go crazy!

J   And what if it never rained again?

Es That would be awful. Everything would dry up. We probably wouldn't even have food.

J   Exactly, and what if it turned 90 degrees in January?

Es Hummmm . . . bet some non-winter people would like that . . . but then we couldn't go sliding, or ice-skating, or make snowmen.

J   What if it was always night and no daylight ever again?

Es You mean we'd go to school in the dark. We probably wouldn't have recess—that's the best part of the day, and dad would SURELY complain about the light bill.

J   Esmerelda, if you think about who made our earth, we don't ever have to worry about those things happening.

Es We don't?

J   God created our earth, and he's very DEPENDABLE.

Es There's that word again.

J   We know that the earth won't stop turning, that rain will fall, that it won't be 90 degrees in January and when morning comes it will be light.

Es *(emphatically)* Boy, I'm glad God never lets us down . . . *(pause—hangs head)* But I let you down, didn't I, Joannie? . . . I'm going to try . . . I want you to know you can DEPEND on me too.

J Let's pray:
Dear God,
We can always DEPEND on you, not only the way you care for the earth, but the way you care for us. Help us to always do what we say we will, so others can depend on us. Amen.

MEMORY MEMO
(DEPENDABILITY IS A BIG WORD)

CINDERELLA—ran away from ball

OCTOPUS—hand

AVOIDING YESTERDAY—clean room
  - stuff doesn't have place
  - more incentive than airlines

LIST:
  - 1. Locate closet
  - 2. Grasp hanger
  - 3. Hold hanger—pick up shirt
  - 4. Insert clothes-hanger
  - 5. Locate pole
  - 6. Hang clothes—repeat steps

DISAPPOINTED DIDN'T DO PART
  - COMPANY
  - DEPENDABILITY IS
    IMPORTANT
  - DEPENDABILITY—BIG WORD

QUESTION:
  - World stopped turning—winter
  - Summer all year—mom's crazy
  - Always night—no daylight
  - recess
  - light bill

GOD IS VERY DEPENDABLE

GOD NEVER LETS US DOWN
  - I want you to know you can
    DEPEND on me too.

ARE YOU BLIND WITH YOUR EYES WIDE OPEN?
(SCRIP. JOHN 9:1-41)

<u>IDEA:</u> *Understanding how others feel*
<u>PROPS:</u> *Blindfold on puppet*

Es I don't think I like this at all! Whose idea is this to put a blindfold on? Where are we?

J Just calm down, Es, we're in front of the church.

Es Where are the kids?

J They are coming down. They all look so nice.

Es Can I see?

J No, not yet. While they are getting settled we'll just talk. You were just in Sunday School weren't you?

Es Uh-huh.

J What did you think of the story of Jonah and the Whale?

Es I thought it was really good.

J What did you learn from the story?

Es I learned that even a whale can't stomach a preacher!

J *(grasped hand over mouth in utter dismay)* Esmerelda! This isn't exactly the place to say that! Boy, this sure isn't our week.

Es Why?

J Yesterday, for example.

Es Oh, yeah.

J I just don't understand why you got in a fight with Todd. How many times have I told you to count to 100 before you do anything?

Es Yeah, but Todd's mother only told him to count to 50!

J And then to top it off, when Todd threw rocks at you . . . why didn't you come and tell me, instead of throwing rocks back at him?

Es It wouldn't have done any good. You couldn't hit the side of a barn!

J *(softly)* Es. Today in the scripture it told about Jesus healing the blindman. That's why I put that blindfold on you. I wanted you to know what it's like not to be able to see.

Es It's awful. This was a terrible idea!

J Tell me . . . how do you feel?

Es Well, I need you to take care of me. I can't see the steps. I can't see the kids. I don't know if it's sunny or gray outside . . . can I come out now?

J OK *(removes the blindfold)*

Es Whew! That's more like it. Hi, kids!

J You know, Esmerelda, even when we can see, we're still blind sometimes.

Es Huh? That doesn't make any sense at all . . . *(repeats)* we can see, but still we're blind?

J Well, how many of you kids have walked in the warm sun, past the green grass, colorful flowers and never really noticed God's beautiful earth?

Es *(nods head)* I even walked past a dollar on the sidewalk. My friend found it instead of me. Now that is REALLY blind!

J Or how many of you had a friend, or brother or sister who cried because their feelings were hurt, and you didn't do anything to help?

Es Oh, oh . . . I'm guilty.

J Or your mom came home so tired and you could've helped tidy up, or care for a baby, or hang up your clothes, and you were too blind to notice?

Es Guilty again . . . how can we have our eyes wide open and still not notice important things?

J We don't have to be REALLY blind to miss so many chances to care about others.

Es *(hangs head)*

J What's the matter, Es?

Es Well, you know that Todd I threw rocks at?

J How could I forget?

Es Well, I guess I was blind.

J What do you mean?

Es Ya see, I heard Todd's dog got run over by a car. And I know that sometimes when you feel sad . . . you get angry real easy.

J So you should've understood why Todd threw rocks.

Es Yeh, I guess so.

J Es, remember what you said when I asked how you felt to be blind?

Es Yeh, I said, "I need you to take care of me."

109

J Well, God's like that . . . he takes care of us when we hit those blind spots in our life when we aren't seeing too clearly. He never quits caring.

Es Wow, it's so good to know that when you goof, you're not out on your tail.

J Hummmmm . . . I guess you could say that. But love is such a special thing and God's love . . . *(slowly)* well, it's just always there. Shall we pray:
Dear God,
Please help us not to be blind to what other people need. But especially may we never be blind to the fact that you are always there whenever we need you.   Amen.

MEMORY MEMO
(ARE YOU BLIND WITH YOUR EYES OPEN)

BLINDFOLD

JONAH AND THE WHALE
    Stomach a preacher
    Not our week

FIGHT WITH TODD
    Rocks
    Side of barn

FEEL LIKE A BLINDMAN
    Need you to care for me
    Can't see steps
    Can't see kids
    Sunny or gray

REMOVE BLINDFOLD
    Even when can't see—are blind sometimes
    Never noticed God's earth
    Walked past a dollar
    Sister cried
    Mother tired

TODD'S DOG—RUN OVER

GOD TAKES CARE OF US WHEN WE HIT BLIND SPOTS

WHEN YOU "GOOF" NOT OUT ON YOUR TAIL

GOD'S LOVE IS ALWAYS THERE

PRAYER

INSIDE VS. OUTSIDE

<u>IDEA</u>: *It is what is on the inside of us that counts.*
<u>PROPS</u>: *Pictures of two houses—one gorgeous, one unpretentious*

Es Hoy Cow, I almost didn't make it to Sunday School this morning . . . I was all tuckered out from starting school.

J Well, I see you made it!

Es Ya, I made it all right, with a huge push from you . . . *(thoughtfully)* but I really didn't want to miss Sunday School today.

J Well, good! Say, I really like your outfit *(Could comment on color or style)*

Es You should, it's one of your K-Mart Blue Light Specials.

J Oh . . . that's right . . . looks great.

Es If you say so . . . hey, Joannie, what do you get if you cross a mosquito with a rabbit?

J C'mon Esmerelda, you know I am never good at these things . . . *(thinking)* What do you get when you cross a mosquito with a rabbit? *(turns to Es)* What?

Es You get BUGS BUNNY.

J Honestly!

Es Now, what would you have if you crossed a giraffe with an ostrich?

J A giraffe with an ostrich . . . got me!

Es Well, I'll tell you this, Joannie, you'd really be "sticking" your neck out!

J Esmerelda! And where may I ask did you collect all this intelligent information?

Es Well, you see, we have this new boy in class. He sits behind me. His name is Luke and he's from _____ *(city, state)*

J He sounds like fun.

Es He is . . . but some of the kids ignore him 'cuz he's on crutches and he can't play ball or anything. I think he's kinda' lonely in a new school and all.

J May I change the subject for a minute? *(turning to Esmerelda)*

Es You're going to do what you want anyway. *(J frowns.)*

111

J   I want to show you something. I have two pictures here, and I want you to tell me where you would rather live. *(shows children and Esmerelda the pictures of the two houses—one gorgeous, one very simple—could describe. After all have seen ask:)*
Okay, let's take a vote. Who would rather live in this beautiful house with the swimming pool? Hands up! Only vote for one now!

Es *I would! I would! (Count votes, including Esmerelda)*

J   Okay, now who would like to live in this smaller house? *(Count hands)*

Es Joannie, that is really a dumb vote. Why would anyone pick the smaller house when they could live in that gorgeous one?

J   All right, what if inside this beautiful house *(hold up)* the mom and dad fought a lot, no one really cared about each other and they never did anything together . . . but, in the smaller house they talked a lot and laughed a lot, played games together, planned vacations, worked together, and had popcorn and apples in front of the fire . . .

Es Joannie, that's not fair. I guess if I was so unhappy and sad . . . a beautiful house wouldn't help much . . . I'd pick the little house . . . I like to play games . . . and I looooove popcorn.

J   *(to children)* How many of you agree with Esmerelda? You see, Es, what I am really getting at, just like those two houses, it's what is on the inside that really matters . . . and people are like that too.

Es What do you mean?

J   You see, so often we judge people by the outside. Are they pretty or handsome, do they have nice clothes or do they wear the "in" name brand of tennis shoes.

Es I get it! You mean like my friend Luke. When the kids judged him by his crutches instead of who he really is inside?

J   Exactly. Sometimes we can miss knowing the nicest friends because we have judged them only by what we see.

Es I guess I certainly don't mind crutches, if Luke doesn't mind the color green. *(color or characteristic of puppet)*

J   You have the idea, Esmerelda. Shall we pray:
Dear God,
As Sunday School begins, help us to look past the outside of our friends, and look inside where we can see their kindness and caring. And Lord, help me to be beautiful inside.
Amen.

MEMORY MEMO
(INSIDE VS. OUTSIDE)

ALMOST DIDN'T MAKE IT
- Push
- Outfit

RIDDLES
- Mosquito—Rabbit
- Giraffe—Ostrich

NEW BOY

CHANGE

TWO PICTURES - where live?

VOTE

BEAUTIFUL
- Mom and Dad fought
- No one cared
- Never did together

SMALLER
- Talked—laughed
- Played games
- Planned vacations
- Worked together
- Popcorn
    -Unhappy, sad—beautiful house wouldn't help
    - Like games & popcorn

INSIDE WHAT MATTER
—People like that
- Pretty
- Handsome
- Clothes
- Tennis shoes

LUKE JUDGED BY CRUTCHES

MISS KNOWING NICE FRIENDS

DON'T MIND CRUTCHES IF HE DOESN'T MIND

THE QUILT

IDEA: *Back to Sunday School (Sept.)*
PROP: *Small quilt with different fabric squares*

J   Esmerelda, can you believe that vacation is over, school has started and today we begin Sunday School?

Es   I wasn't sure if I was quite ready for this. You know at school this week our teacher said, "At the beginning of the school year we assign students to a specific locker. We expect students to remain IN the lockers to which they are assigned."

J   Yes?

Es   Holy Cow, it's gonna be an uninteresting year . . . spending it in my locker!

J   Esmerelda!

Es Then we had to go to the school nurse and she looked thru everyone's hair to make sure they didn't have any HEADLIGHTS.

J Es, I think she was looking for head lice.

Es Guess that's right. Then my teacher said we were in the class of 2004. *(looks at Joannie)* Is that true? I've been counting and counting and I JUST don't think there are that many kids in my class!

J Esmerelda, she is talking about the year you graduate.

Es Whew, I'm glad I finally figured that one out! Hey, Joannie, what have you got there?

J *(Joannie holds up a quilt)* Isn't this pretty? Who knows what it is? *(Let kids answer)*

Es It's patches all sewn together.

J And what do we call that? *(Get QUILT answer)* Coming back to Sunday School is like this quilt.

Es Joannie . . . I don't get it!

J See all the different colors and different designs. *(Kids could point to favorite color, or favorite design)*

Es I like green, where's green . . . see there's green.

J Es, wait your turn, *(after children have pointed to favorite one)* See how you each like different colors, you like different designs . . . each of you is different just like each one of these squares is different.

Es Are you saying I'm a square?

J Esmerelda, of course not! When each of you walks into your class today, each one of you is different and unique.

Es Well, Arnold, he certainly is dif . . . *(Joannie closes puppet's mouth)*

J No names, Es. And different is what makes our classes interesting. What if everyone was quiet like _____ or outspoken like you, Es?

Es Holy Cow!

J Our world is so fascinating because people come in DIFFERENT colors . . . they wear DIFFERENT clothes . . . they make their living doing DIFFERENT jobs . . . and they come from DIFFERENT families.

Es That's cool!

J   But really we are all here for the SAME reason.

Es   HUH?

J   Why are we here, Es?

Es   *(thinks a minute)* To learn about Jesus . . . to learn about God.

J   Exactly *(points to stitches around each square on the quilt)* See this stitch that holds these squares together . . . that's like God's love. Even though we all are different as these squares are, this thread of God's love holds us together.

Es   That's neat, Joannie, we really ARE the same.

J   *(looks at Esmerelda)*

Es   We all need each other . . . and we all need God's love.

J   Shall we pray:
Dear God,
You have made some of us tall, some short; some with blond hair, some with black or brown; some like to draw, some like to play soccer and some have big families, some have small . . . but we all need you, God, you help us to understand that each of us is very special to you. Thank-you for this new year of Sunday School.
Amen.

MEMORY MEMO
(THE QUILT)

TODAY BEGIN SUNDAY SCHOOL
- Expect student to remain IN locker assigned
- Holy Cow—uninteresting year
- Headlights—head lice
- Class of 2004—not that many kids in class

QUILT
- Different colors and designs
- Where's green?
- Each different like each square of quilt
- Different and unique

DIFFERENCES MAKE CLASSES INTERESTING
- Quiet like _____
- Outspoken like you, Es

WORLD FASCINATING
because people:
- come in different colors
- wear different clothes
- different jobs
- different families

HERE FOR SAME REASON—Learn about Jesus
- Stitch holds quilt together— like God's love
- Even tho different like each square—thread of God's love holds us together

GOD'S HUG

J   GOOD MORNING, Es!

Es   Hi, Joannie.

J   Had a good week?

Es   Guess so . . . in math we were talking about numbers we remembered.

J   Like what?

Es   Well, I decided that you remember different numbers depending on how old you are.

J   For example?

Es   Well, senior citizens remember their social security number, Mom remembers her Visa number, and people under 15 know all the cable channels.

J   Interesting . . . and school is going good?

Es   I guess . . . Yesterday I was telling some of my friends about not being able to find my locker. Then Richard came by, Lou my friend likes him! I sure don't know why! She wasn't even listening to my story. Boy, when I don't have someone to listen . . . I'm sunk!

J   I can certainly believe that! We all have experienced the frustration of being with another person and feeling that other person isn't paying attention to us, Es.

Es   You know, we talked about prayer in Sunday School . . . and sometimes I don't know if God is listening.

J   Sometimes our problem with God is that we cannot see Him. But just because a blind person cannot see the sun, it doesn't mean the sun isn't there. And just because we cannot see God does not mean that He isn't there.

Es   What really is prayer, Joannie?

J   Prayer is knowing that someone is there, someone who loves me very much. Prayer is a loving answer to that someone.

Es Huh?

J Prayer is not WHAT we do, but WHO we meet.

Es What?

J Let me say that again. Prayer is not WHAT we do, but WHO we meet.

Es So we shouldn't just pray, but we should talk . . . to God.

J Exactly, Es . . . have you ever run and hugged your mom, your dad or a grandma or grandpa?

Es Sure! Gramma gives huge hugs.

J That's kinda' what prayer is like.

Es A hug?

J Yes, a hug. Next time you see someone bright and smiling run and hug someone . . . you will have an idea of what prayer is supposed to be like.

Es My teacher says many people think they are too busy to pray.

J What do you think?

Es Well, I guess we get too busy to eat breakfast, to do homework, to clean my room, to set the table, to mow the lawn. Guess prayer could be on that list too.

J We can pray anywhere, Es, on the bus, walking to school, at lunch . . . anywhere. And we should ask God to be with us, but we should remember to thank him for all he's done.

Es And we should listen . . . God must feel bad when we don't listen just like I did.

J I'm sure he does, Es . . . God has created us . . . he wants to share his life and love with us always. So prayer is how we send our love to him.

Es Like a hug . . .

J Yes, Es, like a hug . . . Shall we pray.
Dear God,
I am glad I can meet you often in prayer. I know You love me. Thank you for your many hugs.
Amen.

117

MEMORY MEMO
(GOD'S HUG)

NUMBERS REMEMBERED
- Seniors—social security
- Moms—Visa
- Kids—Cable Channels

TELLING STORY TO FRIENDS
- Not listening
- not paying attention

PRAYER
- Don't know if God is listening
- Just because can't see—doesn't mean isn't there
- Is knowing someone is there
- Is a loving answer to that someone
Prayer is not what we do, but who we meet
- Shouldn't just pray . . . talk to God
- Grandma or Grandpa—hugs
- Prayer is like a hug.

People too busy:
- to eat breakfast
- to do homework
- to clean room
- to set table
- to mow lawn
- to pray

CAN PRAY ANYTIME AND ANYWHERE

GOD WANTS TO SHARE HIS LIFE AND LOVE WITH US

LIKE A HUG

TOO MANY BOSSES!

<u>IDEA:</u> *Esmerelda doesn't appreciate teachers and parents telling her what to do.*
<u>PROPS:</u> *Hat, Large shirt for Esmerelda*

J   Boy, Esmerelda, you certainly look great. That new top is neat.

Es   It's "one size fits all."

J   Ok?

Es   That usually means it doesn't fit anybody!

J   And I especially like that hat.

Es   I bought this hat two years ago . . . I had it washed twice, exchanged it in a restaurant once and it still looks as good as new.

J   Really? Do you like school?

Es   Of course, Joannie, if it wasn't for school we wouldn't get any holidays.

J   Did you have a good week in school?

Es   It was okay . . . but I need you to help me with something.

J   What's that?

Es How to whisper without moving my lips.

J   Esmerelda! Listen, with a new school year, it's like a new beginning and I think that this year you should decide that you are going to do great job, and NO short-cuts.

Es What do you mean?

J   That means doing your own work.

Es C'mon, Joannie, you parents always come up with all these ideas of what we kids should do.

J   Like what, Esmerelda?

Es Like when you asked me to share my bike.

J   I thought it was only fair, with two of your friends wanting to ride it. I want your friends to think you are a good kid.

Es Then you always ask me to stay out of the street. You know that is the best place to play ball!

J   I care about you, Esmerelda. I don't want anything to happen to you.

Es And my teachers aren't any better. They have all these ridiculous rules like don't chew gum, single file, tie your shoes, and only blue gym shorts, red is a MUCH better color, and a demerit if your work is late . . . and hurry . . . everyone tells you to hurry!

J   Welcome to the real world, Es.

Es I don't like having so many bosses. Why can't I be my own boss?

J   Esmerelda, do you remember when we saw that movie about the bear, and how the mother bear taught the cub how to hunt for food, protect itself against other wild animals . . . just how to survive?

Es Yeah, that was neat!

J   Well, parents and teachers are like that . . . we try to teach you the things that will make your life safe and happy. That means teaching you to make good choices.

Es You mean you aren't being bossy . . . just trying to teach me something?

J   Right.

Es Could've fooled me!

J Esmerelda, can I tell you something?

Es Sure.

J Would you believe that we parents give up many things for our kids?

Es Really?

J In order for parents to get to conferences, musical concerts, or sporting events, it means missing work or not being about to do things we had planned . . . but we want to be there, Es. As parents we're proud of our kids . . . have you ever noticed that we are really your best cheerleaders?

Es You are, Joannie . . . I know you are . . . you always ask about my day, how it went, how my spelling test was . . . I don't ask about your day very often. I should . . . shouldn't I?

J That's okay. *(hesitates)* Well . . . yes . . . it would be nice. I guess we parents need to know that we are doing okay too.

Es *(thinks)* Joannie, when you make cookies . . . which isn't often enough . . . but when you do . . . they are absolutely the best!

J Hey, thanks, Es. Shall we pray:
Dear God:
Thank you so very much for teachers and moms and dads who really care about us. They are always there to cheer us on. Help us to understand . . . rules are made because parents and teachers care about us and love us. Amen.

MEMORY MEMO
(TOO MANY BOSSES)

NEW TOP—One size fits all

HAT—Washed—exchanged restaurant

SCHOOL—Whisper without moving lips
- Great job
- No short cuts!

PARENTS' IDEAS
- Share bike
- Stay out of street

TEACHERS
- Don't chew gum
- Single file
- Tie shoes
- Only blue gym shorts (red—better)
- Demerit if work late
- Hurry!

1 TOO MANY BOSSES
- BEAR—movie
- Teach—to make good choices

PARENTS
- Give up things
- The best Cheerleaders
Parents need to know doing okay
- Cookies
- Absolutely the best!

STANDING ON THE PROMISES

IDEA: *God's promises to us*
PROPS: *Paper taped to bottom of shoes*

Es Hi, kids.

J Good morning. Don't they look great?

Es They sure do, and I have a riddle . . . what did the bird say when his cage broke?

J *(repeat)* What did the bird say when his cage broke? Got me!

Es Cheap! Cheap!

J Oh, really!

Es I have another one!

J Es . . . listen . . .

Es Just a minute, Joannie, I have another riddle.

J Es, you know I can never get your ridd . . .

Es *(interrupts)* Why did the football coach run into the phone booth?

J Why did the football coach run into the phone booth, Esmerelda?

Es To get his quarterback.

J *(look of oh, really)* Esmerelda, what on earth do you have taped on your feet?

Es Those are promises.

J Promises?

Es Yep.

J *(Joannie picks up foot and reads)* Let's see this one says I will do my homework every night. That's a good one . . . what's on the other foot . . . *(lifts foot and reads)* I will put my bike away, clean my room and take out the garbage. This is very good too.

Es All the stuff I have to do . . . I might as well be married.

J Esmerelda, these are good, but why are you wearing these on your feet?

Es We sang this song, *Standing on the Promises* and I just wanted to see if it works . . .

J Es, un-huh, that isn't going to do it.

Es Why not . . . the song . . .

J But the song isn't talking about promises to other people, it's talking about God's promises to us.

Es You mean God promises us stuff?

J He certainly does.

Es Like what?

J In Matthew 18:20, it says "when two or three come together in my name I'm with you." Hebrews 13:5 says, "I will never leave or forsake you."

Es I like that one, Joannie. Can you write it down for me? Then I can wear one of *God's* promises on my shoe.

J Esmerelda, when we talk about standing on the promises, it doesn't mean standing on them with our shoes, it means standing on them with our faith, what we believe.

Es How do you do that?

J You see, it's learning to trust God. When we have problems, we need to remember that God is with us and cares about us.

Es So that is what that song is about!

J Yes.

Es Joannie, would you help me get these promises off my shoes? I put them on with super glue!

J Super Glue! Let's pray:
Dear God:
We know you have promised to love us. You never forget your promises to us. We do thank you for being so good. Amen.

Sing: Standing on the Promises

MEMORY MEMO
(STANDING ON THE PROMISES)

CAGE BROKE
    Cheap

FOOTBALL COACH
    Quarterback

TAPED FEET

READ:
    Homework
    Bike Away
    Clean Room
    Garbage

MARRIED

GOOD—Why wear on feet?
    Song: Stand on Promises
    Not promises—people
    Promises from God

God promises stuff
    Matt 18:20—Two, three together—with you
    Hebrews 13:5—I will never leave, forsake you

Wear God's promises

When talk about *STANDING ON PROMISES* . . .
    Not stand on with shoes
    Stand on with faith

Learning to trust God—Problems
    God loves us—cares
    Song about

Promises off shoes
Super Glue

PRAYER

SOMETIMES WE NEED TO WAIT

<u>IDEA:</u> *Patience*
<u>PROP:</u> *Tulip, daffodil bulbs*

Es   Joannie, what is a witch's favorite subject in school?

J   What?

Es   SPELLING! You know Halloween is coming soon . . . here's another one: *(say in scary tone)* What do ghosts and ghouls wear in the rain?

J   Okay, Es, you know how I love these riddles of yours . . . let's hear it!

Es   Booooo-oots and Ghoul-oshes.

J   Listen, aren't you a little early here?

Es   I wish Halloween was here.

J   Goodness, Es, it'll be here before you know it.

Es   And I wish Christmas was only a week away.

J   Esmerelda, don't ever wish that. I certainly wouldn't be ready . . . shopping, decorating, cards, baking . . . I'd like a little more time, please.

123

Es And I wish I was old enough to drive. I hate always waiting for you to take me.

J You drive quite well from the backseat, Es.

Es And I wish I had enough money to buy anything I want whenever I want!

J You get an allowance.

Es Yeah, but I have to put half of it in the bank, and the other half never covers much at all. I could use a raise.

J Esmerelda! Why are you so impatient? You want everything right now. Sometimes you just have to wait.

Es Waiting doesn't fit my personality.

J Esmerelda, do you remember what we did this week?

Es Let's see . . . we ate a few meals, watched a little TV . . .

J No . . . no . . . what did we do that we don't usually do each week?

Es Oh . . . *(looks at Joannie)* you mean in the garden?

J Yes.

Es We planted bulbs.

J *(show children bulbs)* Kids, this is what we put in the ground.

Es *(Esmerelda looks at bulb)* Funny lookin' thing, isn't it? That one will be a daffodil . . .

J How about this one, Es?

Es You said that would be a tulip . . . I thought it was a silly time to plant 'cuz they would all freeze and smother in the snow.

J But the snow is like a blanket. It keeps them warm all winter. Then what?

Es Well . . . we have to WAIT all winter, and in the spring they will bloom into beautiful flowers. I can hardly wait.

J But we do have to wait, don't we?

Es *(Slowly)* Yeah, one more thing that I have to wait for.

J Esmerelda, do you think that might be God's way of teaching us to be patient, to wait and hope for spring and its beautiful flowers after a long cold winter?

Es I guess if I got everything I wanted right how, I wouldn't have anything to wait for . . . would I? Nothing to look forward to . . .

J Let me tell you about a great singer. She worked very hard, she practiced and practiced, she succeeded and failed. Finally after a concert she was a hit! And the newspaper came out and said she was an "Overnight Success."

Es Overnight Success?

J Meaning after that concert she would finally be well-known.

Es Holy Cow! Just overnight she was famous.

J Well, not really. When a reporter asked about her "overnight success," she said, "an overnight success usually takes about 20 years."

Es Twenty years! That long?

J We need to learn to wait for good things to happen, but in the meantime we need to practice and learn and get ready . . . in other words—live each day to our best!

Es *(with feelings)* You're right, Joannie. SOMETIMES WE JUST NEED TO WAIT!

J Shall we pray: Dear God,
Help us to understand that some of the things that we want so badly take time. May we be like the tulip bulb in the earth that waits for Spring. Thank you God for always waiting with us.   Amen.

MEMORY MEMO
(SOMETIMES WE NEED TO WAIT)

*WITCHES FAVORITE SUBJECT—*Spelling

GHOSTS AND GHOULS WEAR
—Boooooots—Ghoul-oshes
- Wish Halloween was here
- Wish Christmas week away
- Wish old enough to drive
- Wish enough money to anything—Raise

WHY SO IMPATIENT?
—Waiting doesn't fit personality

DID THIS WEEK?
- Planted bulbs
- Wait all winter until spring

GOD'S WAY—TEACHING PATIENCE

NOTHING TO LOOK FORWARD TO

OVERNIGHT SUCCESS—20 years

NEED TO WAIT FOR GOOD THINGS TO HAPPEN

LAITY SUNDAY

J   Es, isn't Fall a great time of year?

Es   Yep, it's that time of year when everyone gets their winter clothes out and comes to church and they have a certain air about them.

J   What's that?

Es   Mothballs!

J   C'mon, Es . . . you've been in school for awhile now, tell me about your week.

Es   It sure was a terrible week.

J   Really . . . why is that?

Es   First, my teacher said that I could pick the teams in gym on Monday, and she wasn't there so Darren got to do it. She was probably out playing golf.

J   Esmerelda, I don't think so . . . maybe she was sick.

Es   Well, then Teresa was 'spose to bring a treat for Scouts . . . and she forgot.

J   So you felt badly.

Es   No . . . I was absolutely furious.

J   Es, I'm sure that you didn't starve.

Es   Then I was going to carry the pumpkin for our Costume Parade . . .

J   Oh, Halloween is coming up . . .

Es   But Mary started to cry 'cuz she wanted to do it, so I said she could . . . but I REALLY wanted to do it myself.

J   That was very nice, Es.

Es   Yeh, nice for Mary, but not for me. I don't like school much this week.

J   Wow, it was disappointing, wasn't it?

Es   I'm not finished . . . then I get to church today and my teacher asked if I could help in the nursery again this year. *(emphatically)* Well, this time Esmerelda is going to pass. This time Esmerelda is going to say "no way." This time . . .

J   Esmerelda . . . why?

Es   I'm always the one they ask:
Esmerelda . . . pick up the blocks
Esmerelda . . . tidy the shelves
Esmerelda . . . help with the treat
Esmerelda . . . would you . . .

J   *(interrupting Es, looking at the children)* Excuse me, Es . . . but kids, do you know what Sunday this is? Do you know what today is? It's a special Sunday. *(Esmerelda is waving arms, trying to get attention, Joannie ignores her, trying to get answer from the children . . . no answer . . . Joannie recognizes Esmerelda)*

J   Okay, Es, what is today?

Es   It is Laity Sunday.

J   How did you know that?

Es   I looked at the script . . . you don't think you did this thing all by yourself, do you?

J   So what does it mean?

Es   Laity means the people of the church, not the pastors . . . that means _____ *(name of pastor)* is out on this one.

J   The church needs everyone to make it strong . . . to survive.

Es   I'm Laity?

J   You sure are . . . the choir needs people or laity to sing . . .

Es   _____ *(choir director)* can do that.

J   We need laity to call on the sick.

Es   _____ *(pastor)* can do that.

J   We need laity to plan church programs.

Es   _____ *(pastor)* can do that.

J   We need laity to help with the youth.

Es   _____ *(Youth pastor)* can do that.

J   Esmerelda . . . they can't possibly do it alone. They need each one of us to do our part . . . that's what makes a great church.

Es You know, Joannie, I almost didn't have a teacher this year . . . no one volunteered.

J That sure would've been awful. You love Sunday School.

Es Well, Mrs. Adams said she'd do it. Guess they raised her salary.

J Esmerelda, they don't get paid. They do it because they care about our church.

Es Joannie, it takes lots of time . . . Lisa, my friend, her mother said her dad really didn't die, he just became President of the Church Council.

J The church is like a family doing chores together. When everyone helps the jobs get done, and what's more it's fun that way.

Es *(pulling away)* Joannie, may I be excused? I have to go.

J Where are you going?

Es I gotta go tell _____ *(Pastor, Education Dir.)* I'll help in the nursery. I sure had a disappointing week, but I don't want anyone in our church to be disappointed . . . not 'cuz of me anyway!

J Great, Esmerelda! Can we pray?

Es Sure. Hey, can I say it today?

J Sure.
Dear God,
Thank you for a great church where everyone helps each other . . . because, God, when you help you feel needed and when you feel needed you feel happy. Amen.

MEMORY MEMO
(LAITY SUNDAY)

WINTER COATS—Mothballs

TERRIBLE WEEK
- Pick teams
- Treat—Scouts
- Carry Pumpkin
- Help in Nursery—ssno wayss

WHY?
- Pick up blocks
- Tidy shelves
- Help—treat

LAITY SUNDAY—Script

LAITY means:
- Choir
- Sick
- Plan
- Youth

No Teacher

President—Church Council—didn't die

Church—Family doing chores together
- Everyone helps—gets done
- Disappointing Week—Not because of me

128

THERMOMETER OR THERMOSTAT?

<u>IDEA:</u> *Attitude*
<u>PROP:</u> *Artwork*

Es I am absolutely disgusted! No one has it together around here except me. Absolutely no one!

J Really?

Es Yes, really.

J Can you clarify things a bit?

Es I certainly can! For example, I forgot my library book, so when it came time to read . . . no book . . . so I had to clean the bookcase. Can you imagine that? I was really mad. Then Dopey Dorothy tripped in the lunchroom and spilled her milk all over my sandwich. Have you ever had peanut-butter float?

J Can't say as I have.

Es Well, I wouldn't recommend it. It really ruins the appetite. Then, take a look at this great piece of artwork. *(picture pinned to hand of puppet—raised for puppeteer to see)* No really, can you believe that my teacher didn't like this? I mean this is a masterpiece like no other.

J *(examines picture)* Hummmmmmmmm.

Es *(Carries on)* This has originality, personality and depth. I can't believe my teacher didn't like it.

J She wrote here . .. *(looking at picture)* Not within the subject suggested. *(looks at Es)* What were you supposed to draw?

Es Oh, she came up with some stupid idea about the early pioneers.

J Well, this looks like a dinosaur riding on a Ferris wheel.

Es *(excited)* See, you understood what I had in mind. Holy Cow, that is much more creative than some old pioneers. And who gave her the authority to be an art critic?

J Esmerelda, you didn't follow directions. You drew a dinosaur instead of pioneers.

Es I'll tell you . . . that was no small trick getting that dinosaur to sit in that Ferris wheel!

J I'd say you are feeling sorry for yourself . . . and complaining. And you do exaggerate the problem sometimes. Maybe you need to change your attitude.

Es My attitude? You mean I'm sky-high on this one?

J No, we're not talking ALTITUDE here *(points up)* . . . we are talking attitude.

Es What's attitude?

J Well, Es, it's how you think about things.

Es Oh, I get it. When things are great, then I'm great; when things are awful, I'm awful.

J Right! You know, Es, life is full of real bummers. Some are small, some are big ones, but our attitude makes all the difference. We can let the circumstances determine our attitude or we can keep a proper attitude and see how it can change the circumstances.

Es I think you lost me.

J Let's see *(thinking)* . . . how can I explain this? You know what a thermometer is, don't you?

Es Yeah, it measures hot if it's hot and cold if it's cold.

J Right . . . if the temperature goes up, the thermometer goes up. If the temperature goes down the thermometer goes down.

Es So?

J All right, do you know what a thermostat is?

Es Sure. We have one in our house. You set it and it keeps the house at that temperature all the time.

J With a thermostat you can create your own climate. If you like it 70 degrees you can set it at 70. If you like the 60's you can set it at 60.

Es Too cold for me! What's the point?

J Well, people are like that.

Es *(Amazed)* Like a thermometer or a thermostat? C'mon, Joannie.

J Yes, some people are like a thermometer. They can only reflect what is going on around them. If everything is falling apart they fall apart. But other people are like thermostats. They choose the proper attitude, and by doing that they change what is around them.

Es God helps you do that, huh?

J He sure does, Esmerelda. Somehow people who keep God in their lives do a better job of being thermostats.

Es That could be, but when that dumb Arnie teases me . . . I can turn into a thermometer real fast! The temperature goes up, pronto!

J Keep working on it, Es. God will be there no matter what.

Es You know what I think?

J What?

Es Well, when people have problems, they forget about God . . . *(thinks)* maybe that's their problem.

J Well said . . . shall we pray:

Dear God,
When those bummers happen, when problems come up, help us to reach out and take your hand. May we be thermostats. I know if I change my thoughts, I can change my world.   Amen.

MEMORY MEMO
(THERMOMETER—THERMOSTAT)

NO ONE HAS IT TOGETHER
- Forgot library book—clean bookcase
- Dorothy tripped—milk sandwich

ARTWORK
- Teacher didn't like
- Originality, personality, depth
- Suppose to draw—pioneers
- Dinosaur Ferris wheel

CHANGE ATTITUDE
- Circumstances determine attitude
- Keep proper attitude

THERMOMETER—measure hot and cold

THERMOSTAT—Keeps temperature where it's set

PEOPLE ARE LIKE THERMOMETERS AND THERMOSTATS
- Reflect what's going on around them
- Choose proper attitude

GOD IN OUR LIVES—BETTER THERMOSTATS
PEOPLE—Problems—Forget about God

131

HALF-COCKED HALLOWEEN

IDEA: *Helping children be compassionate*
PROP: *Puppet is dressed in a Big-Bird mask and colorful hair*

J   Esmerelda, you look absolutely ridiculous, what is that get-up?

Es   Shhhhhhhhh! I'm hiding!

J   Hiding? From what?

Es   Well, I figured if I had this disguise on, no one would find me. And there are two things I always wanted . . . to have colorful hair and be famous like Big Bird.

J   Esmerelda!

Es   Will you quit calling me that. How can I hide when you keep uncovering my cover. You ruined everything. Now they all know that I'm Esmerelda.

J   Well, as long as I blew it, you might as well take this foolish looking mask off. *(Removes hair and mask)* What I'd like to know is why you're hiding.

Es   Well, it's a long story . . . see last night I went to this Halloween Party. My friend had it at his house.

J   I see.

Es   We did all the great stuff, games, duck for apples, some excitement too.

J   Really?

Es   Yeah, my friend Nancy, she swallowed a nickel.

J   That's awful. I 'spose they called a doctor right away!

Es   Nope. My friend's mom said to call _____ *(pastor's name)*

J   What? Pastor _____?

Es   Yeah, she said Pastor _____ can get money out of anyone! Then some kid at the Halloween Party came up to me and said that I look just like you.

J   *(proudly)* Well, how nice. What did you say?

Es   Nothing. He was a lot bigger than me.

J   Esmerelda, I'll let that pass because we haven't gotten to why you were hiding in this disguise.

Es   Well, after we ate we went out Trick or Treating, and the real fun began when those little kids came by in their costumes.

J   Fun for whom?

Es   Fun for me. We took some of their candy 'cuz we were kinda' old to Trick or Treat. We threw corn. It was fun.

J   Did you get hit with the corn, Esmerelda?

Es   Of course not. I was doing the throwing. It was great fun.

J   I saw you. *(Es looks shocked, then acts rather cool)*

Es   You haven't said a word about how good I looked in my costume.

J   That's because I saw others too. I saw Todd, and he didn't seem to be having a good time.

Es   Aw, he's just a little kid. No one pays much attention to him.

J   That's just it. Nobody does pay much attention to him. He's shy, he's lonely. He dropped his candy when he fell. He didn't have mittens, and his hands were cold. The corn you were throwing was getting down his collar. He was miserable.

Es   *(sheepishly)* All of a sudden I noticed he was really crying! And then I felt really ashamed.

J   I did notice how the other kids let up when they saw you go over and help him find his candy.

Es   It just didn't seem right. I guess I need to take a good look at whose side I'm on. It's not too smart to have fun while hurting someone else.

J   I'm glad you feel that way. I get it now . . . you felt guilty so you thought you could hide behind that mask.

Es   *(hangs head)* Well . . . I guess I did, but I realize it really didn't help much. I have to live with myself and I felt awful inside. It came back to haunt me this morning.

J   This morning? What do you mean?

Es   Well, in Sunday School a kid fell off the chair and everyone laughed except me.

133

J   Well, that was very nice of you. Who was the kid?

Es   Me! I guess I learned a lot this weekend.

J   How's that?

Es   You just feel better inside when you care about others. When my friends and I only cared about OUR fun . . . it just didn't seem right.

J   I'm glad you feel that way, Es.

Es   Guess God must've been disappointed in me.

J   We just have to keep trying, Es. We all make mistakes. Maybe that's why we are here today, to remind us to care about all people.

Es   Can I pray today?

J   Sure.

Es   Dear God:
     Forgive us when we forget to be kind. Thank you for parents, teachers, friends and pastors that really do care about us. Help us to show love to others as they have shown love to us. Amen.

MEMORY MEMO
(HALF-COCKED HALLOWEEN)

HIDING
- No one find me
- Always wanted famous like Big Bird

WHY HIDING?
- Halloween Party
- Games
- Duck apples
- Excitement—Nancy swallowed nickel
- looked just like you
- bigger than me

TRICK OR TREATING
- Took candy
- Threw corn
- Todd—Shy, lonely, dropped candy
- Crying—I felt ashamed
- Others let up when you helped
- "didn't seem right"

NOT TOO SMART TO HAVE FUN WHILE HURTING SOMEONE

CAME BACK TO HAUNT ME
- Kid fell off chair
- Me!

GOD DISAPPOINTED IN ME

WHY HERE TODAY—Remind us to care about all people

TITHING
MALACHI 3:10

IDEA: *Stewardship and Tithing*
PROPS: *Four or five men's ties hanging around puppet's neck*

Es   Boy, it sure is a gray day . . . not a sky in the clouds.

J   Guess that kinda' comes with November, Es.

Es   Joannie, if our house gets covered with snow, will we all be under the weather?

J   Guess that's one way of putting it. I do know this is the time of year when you children leave the doors open that you slammed all summer.

Es   *(Rather matter-a-fact)* Seems a bad habit never disappears easily, it's an "undo-it-yourself project."

J   That's a different twist.

Es   We had fun in Sunday School. Our teacher asked if anyone knew who defeated the Philistines.

J   Did you know?

Es   Well, Dumb Dorothy thought the Philistines were in the NFL!

J   *(laughs)* Really?

Es   We also talked about money.

J   Money? Tell me.

Es   Seeing as the church is talking about all this Stewardship stuff lately . . . my teacher says the money is for God, but how do we get this money up to heaven and what does God do with it? It is for him, isn't it?

J   Yes, Es.

Es   What does God need money for? He doesn't have to buy stuff, he has everything he needs . . . so I went and asked Mr. _____ *(name of usher or finance person who takes care of money)*

J   What did he say?

135

Es He said the church tries to use the money for things that God wants them to.

J Did he say what that was?

Es He said he was sure God wanted us to use the money here on earth to help people, to build churches, to send missionaries and many good things.

J It takes lots of money to do all those things, Es.

Es That's what Mr. _____ said.

J Es, I hate to change the subject, but ever since we came up here I have been so curious. What on earth are you doing with all those ties draped around your neck?

Es I'm collecting them. My Friend Lou, she collected over a dozen. I took a few from dad's closet. He has so many he won't miss them . . .

J Are you sure about that?

Es . . . and Mr. _____ *(someone in church)* he gave me his right off his neck. He said he didn't like it anyway. He said not to say anything to his wife.

J Sure good you didn't say anything! *(rolls eyes)* So what is this? Do you hope to have the world's largest tie collection?

Es Joannie, of course not. This is God's business.

J God's business? And just what does collecting all these ties have to do with God? Does the Bible say anything about gathering up ties?

Es Yeah, it does.

J It does? Where?

Es Our teacher read it to us in Malachi 3:10. It said, "Bring ye all the tithes into the storehouse" . . . now I just have to find the storehouse.

J Es, I think the confusion here is with the word "tithes" . . . you see, the word is tithes, not ties. They are spelled differently. *(Reaches over and picks up tie on Esmerelda's neck)* This is spelled T-I-E, and the tithe in the Bible is spelled T-I-T-H-E.

Es First we have a Sunday School lesson and now we are watching Sesame Street! *(change voice)* And this program is brought to you by the #6 and the letter T!

J Es, do you know the difference?

Es You just said they were spelled different.

J That's right, but the tithe in the Bible isn't something you wear around your neck.

Es It isn't?

J When the Bible says to bring your tithe in to the storehouse, it means to bring one-tenth of all you earn into the Lord's house.

Es The church?

J Yes. You see, Es, if you earn a dollar, one dime should go to God; or if you earn $5.00, then $.50 should go to God.

Es That's a lot!

J If you love your church, you will be generous. *(say following slowly)* It has been said that you can give without loving, but you can't love without giving.

Es So our love for God is by giving to our church?

J Exactly . . . in the Bible it says God loves a cheerful giver.

Es Well, it isn't just in the Bible. Mr. _____ *(head of Stewardship)* says a cheerful giver makes his job a LOT easier.

J *(smiles)* You bet! A lot of people have a hard time giving, but somehow it always comes back to us, Es, and look at all God has given us. We'll never be able to out give God!

Es Holy Cow, that would be impossible! . . . Hey, Joannie, I have to go.

J You do?

Es Yeah, I have a few ties to return!

J Let's pray:
God,
We are happy for a chance to show our love and gratefulness to You through our gifts and offering.
Amen.

MEMORY MEMO
(TITHING)

Not a sky in the clouds
Snow—will we be under the weather?
Doors open you slammed all summer

Philistines—NFL

MONEY
- Money for God
- How get money to heaven
- What does God need money for?
- He doesn't have to buy stuff—has all needs

USHER
- says church uses money for things God wants them to
- Use money to help people here on earth.

TIES
- Curious
- Lou collected—dozen
- Dad's closet
- Right off neck—don't tell wife
- World's largest collection

TIES HAVE TO DO WITH GOD?
- Does Bible say anything about gathering ties?
- Malachi 3:10—"Bring tithes into storehouse"
- Spelled differently

Sunday School—Sesame Street
- Tithe in Bible isn't something wear—neck
- Tithe is 1/10th of what you earn
- $1 . . . .10 should go to God

SAID: You can give without loving, but you can't love without giving.
- God loves cheerful giver
- Never be able to out give God

COUNT YOUR BLESSINGS
SCRIPTURE: I KINGS 17:8-16

<u>IDEA</u>: *Stewardship*

Es *(Clears throat rather noisily)*

J Esmerelda, really! Do you have to do that here?

Es Where's the pastor today?

J He's here, but I'm really surprised. You are rather hard on the pastor sometimes.

Es I'm amazed he's preaching again after what happened last Sunday.

J What do you mean?

Es Well, you see, this lady *(could give name)* in the congregation forgot to turn the oven down under her roast so she wrote a note for the usher to give to her husband.

J   Did he give it to her husband?

Es   No, the usher misunderstood and thought the note was 'sposed to go to the preacher. He delivered it to _____ *(pastor's name)*

J   Well, what did the note say?

Es   It said, "Please go home and turn off the gas."

J   *(hand over mouth)* Oh no!

Es   You know, Joannie, I think I'm getting a little tired of this political campaign. They are conducting it like a well-run grocery meat department.

J   How's that?

Es   You have your choice of bologna!

J   Esmerelda, I'm sure they are sincere.

Es   Well, they are both trying to eliminate poverty, which is ridiculous. That's all some of us have left.

J   I don't believe in political jokes.

Es   Neither do I. TOO many of them are getting elected!

J   Es, how about we leave the ministers and politicians in peace. How was your week?

Es   Not so good. Everything went wrong.

J   Really, I'm sorry to hear that. You've been having a few of those lately.

Es   We had this test with dumb questions like . . . "What is the greatest single disaster recorded in the 20th century?"

J   I 'spose that was a World War. What was your answer?

Es   I wrote . . . my bedroom!

J   *(laughs)* I might be inclined to agree with you.

Es   Then I tried out for the school play. I wanted to be the leading lady.

J   How did that turn out?

Es   Awful! Do you know what that director said?

J   What?

Es   She thought I would be very helpful with costumes. Can you believe that? Costumes!

J   Why did you want to have the lead?

Es   So I could be up in front where everyone could see me, and think how great I am!

J   Well, at least you're honest! But Es, do you realize that you have complained about everything this morning? You have complained about the campaign, tests at school, and now about not getting the part in the school play. Maybe you need to count your blessings . . . seeing the good. Take the campaign. What's good about it?

Es   We DO live in a free country and we CAN elect who we want.

J   Many countries are not free, Es. We are so fortunate. What about school?

Es   I really do like to learn. I'm glad I have a school to go to each day.

J   And what good do you see in the school play?

Es   I still wanted the lead, but it would be a dull play without the costumes and I have some good ideas.

J   In costumes you have to work in the background, but you can make a big difference like in the scripture today. This woman didn't even have enough food for one meal, but she gave all she had to a stranger and God blessed her with more than enough food.

Es   *(disbelief)* Why did she do that?

J   No one knew she gave all she had. She gave in a simple, quiet way, because she had been blessed and so should we . . . we should give just because we are grateful.

Es   I'm grateful to live in this country, grateful to learn, grateful to be head of costumes!

J   You got the idea, Esmerelda.

Es   I guess God loves a cheerful giver . . . that is unless she brags about it!

140

J Shall we pray:
Dear God:
Thank you that we have a chance to work in the background and make a difference. May we give out of gratefulness.
Amen.

MEMORY MEMO
(COUNT YOUR BLESSINGS)

HAPPENED LAST SUNDAY
- Usher—note to husband
- "Go home and turn off the gas"

POLITICAL CAMPAIGN
- Well-run meat dept.
- Choice of bologna
- Eliminate poverty—all have left
- Don't believe in political jokes
  —too many getting elected

HOW WAS YOUR WEEK?
- Dumb question—greatest disaster
  —bedroom
- School play—leading lady—costumes

COMPLAINED ABOUT EVERYTHING
- Campaign
- Tests at school
- Not getting part in play

NEED TO COUNT YOUR BLESSINGS
- Live in free country
- Have a school to attend each day
- Dull without costumes

GIVE BECAUSE WE ARE GRATEFUL

GOD LOVES A CHEERFUL GIVER . . .
UNLESS SHE BRAGS ABOUT IT!

CONTRAPMAJIG

<u>IDEA:</u> *Appreciation of others' efforts*
<u>PROPS:</u> *- Use two puppets—need three different voices*
- Contrapmajig (board with many different shapes nailed to it)
- Club Flag

J Good morning, Esmerelda.

Es *(Rather dejected reply)* Hi.

J Goodness, you don't sound too perky today.

Es I'm not . . . don't even have a joke today.

J Really . . . not even one of those awful riddles? Something must've happened.

Es You can say that again.

J Esmerelda, what on earth happened?

141

Es Well, first off we went on this field trip at school, and I wanted to sit by the window on the bus . . .

J I 'spose you got a seat by the aisle?

Es No, I didn't get a seat at all . . . I had to go with the teacher in her car.

J How come?

Es Well, I was the last one out because the teacher had to talk to me.

J She had to talk to you?

Es *(said sheepishly)* Yeh, I was sorta bothering this boy who sits behind me and my teacher said I better watch my step.

J Really?

Es But I told her that was hard to do when I was sitting down.

J Esmerelda!

Es But the worst thing was I have been working all week on this project.

J Esmerelda . . . when you miss your favorite TV programs for a whole week . . . and then you passed up Susie's slumber party . . . boy, something was really important. What was it?

Es I made something . . . it's over there. *(Joannie picks up a conglomeration of wood pieces in different shapes nailed to a board. Joannie holds it up for children to see)*

J Does it have a name?

Es It's a CONTRAPMAJIG!

J *(said slowly)* A con . . . trap . . . ma . . . jig?

Es Yeah, it's a combination of a contraption and a thing-a-ma-jig.

J Hummmmm, that's interesting.

Es When I gave it to my friend Judy and she asked what it was, and when I told her it was a contrapmajig, she said, "A what?"

J It is different, Es.

Es I told her I didn't have any plans or blueprints, I just made it! She looked at it and said it was WEIRD, and if it was a toy it sure was a stupid one.

J   I 'spose you felt pretty bad after spending all that time?

Es   She said she couldn't use it and told me to check around and see if someone else could use it . . . Gee, I thought she'd be surprised . . . guess she didn't like it . . . I never thought she'd think it was stupid. I thought she would be excited that I had made it for her.

J   Maybe one of your other friends would appreciate it?

Es   Well, I showed it to Sally, and she said that it looked like something out of Star Wars.

J   Did she want it?

Es   Well, when I asked her, she said it would be hard to carry home and she had to go home and watch cartoons.

J   I'm sorry, Es.

Es   I thought that maybe Alvia would like it, but I'm scared to even show it to her.

J   Well, why don't I set this contrapmajig right here and get her.

(At this point Joannie sets the contrapmajig on a stool in front where both puppets can see it, and slips into the other puppet and brings her out. As you are doing this, Esmerelda could be mumbling things like, "I know she won't like it." "It's no use." If you don't care to use another puppet, Es could just tell the following experience)

ALVIA: Hi, Joannie, Hi, Esmerelda!

Es   *(said hesitantly)* Alvia . . . I wanted you to know how much I appreciate you . . . I made something I want you to have . . . it's called a contrapmajig.

ALVIA: Wow, you made this yourself . . . without a kit . . . this is something else! This must've taken hours!

Es   Most of the week. That's why I couldn't go to Susie's party with all you guys.

ALVIA: And you want to give it to me after spending all those hours on it?

Es   Sure.

ALVIA: This would be so neat in my hamster cage. He'd love it! He'd have a ball climbing around on it. This is super.

Es   *(Surprised)* Gosh, I never thought of that.

ALVIA: You know the club flag we made, Es? We've been trying to figure out how to mount it. This is perfect. We can just stick the pole in here. *(points to spot)*

Es Gosh, you're right. *(gets excited)* I'm a genius!

J Who's got the club flag?

(At this time one of the children could put the flag into the stand or contrapmajig)

J It's perfect. *(reads the flag)* Esmerelda and Alvia's Club for the above average? *(then looks at both puppets)* You've got to be kidding!

Es Don't go getting all bent out of shape, Joannie . . . Alvia and I are the only members.

ALVIA: *(to Esmerelda)* Are you sure that you want me to have this, Esmerelda?

Es I'm really happy you want it . . . sure I want you to have it!

ALVIA: That's great. C'mon, I want to show some of my friends. They'll be so jealous . . . I'll be the sole owner of a HANDSOME HAMSTER HANG-OUT!

J Shall we pray:
God:
Thank you for those who take the time to do special things for us. May we always appreciate their efforts by saying "thank-you." There is joy in giving and there is joy in receiving . . . thank you, Lord, for letting us experience that joy.   Amen.

MEMORY MEMO
(CONTRAPMAJIG)

NO JOKE TODAY
- What happened?
- Field trip—sit by window—teacher
- Watch my step
- Project
- missed favorite TV
- Susie's slumber party

CONTRAPMAJIG
- COMB: contraption and thing-a-ma-jig
- Judy—"What is it?"—Weird
- Sally—looked like something—Star Wars
- Alvia—Wow! "taken hours"
     - Give it to me!
     - So neat in my hamster cage
- Hold club flag
- Hold club flag
- "I'm a genius!"

FLAG—"Esmerelda and Alvia's Club for the Above Average
- Only members
- Don't get bent out of shape

HANDSOME HAMSTER HANG-OUT!!!

144

MORE THAN A DRUMSTICK

IDEA: *Thanksgiving*

Es   *(humming tune to self)* I made up a song.

J   Never knew you could do that.

Es   *(Sings—tune: "Over the river and thru the woods")*
Out in the kitchen the day begins,
Thanksgiving day is here.
The relatives a comin', "say" they're quite a few,
Oh my goodness, so much to do.

Turkey and rolls and pumpkin pie,
Isn't it great, oh my?
Hurrah, hurrah the game . . . it's time,
I wish this tummy wasn't mine!
(Sing above line slowly as if full tummy)

J   I didn't know you wrote songs.

Es   Only when I get top dollar!

J   Sounds like you are excited about Thanksgiving.

Es   Of course . . . Turkey . . . dressing . . . cranberries . . . yummm . . .

J   Is that all you think about is food?

Es   Yep! I'm sure glad a long time ago when America was born that the Indians and Pilgrims got together and planned this huge feast. What a GREAT idea . . . only we've added one thing to the menu.

J   What's that?

Es   ALKA SELTZER!

J   Alka Seltzer, Esmerelda! Speaking of food, your Aunt Nancy said she hates the thought of being on a diet this time of year.

Es   Well, just consider it her penalty for exceeding the FEED limit!

J   *(Gives Es a surprised look—repeats)* Feed Limit! And Es, you'll get to see your newest cousin. Uncle Joe and Aunt Dorothy will have their new baby.

Es   Well, Joannie, there's a lot of things they needed worse!

145

J *(Joannie puts hand to mouth in a "oh my goodness" look)* Everyone says the new baby looks just like her dad, your Uncle Joe.

Es Yeah, but what does it matter, as long as it's healthy.

J Listen, Esmerelda, when all the relatives are here I want you to show some consideration.

Es *(slowly)* OOOOOOOOOOkay, I guess consideration for others means taking a wing instead of a drumstick.

J Something like that. *(looks at Es)* But there is something so special about Thanksgiving, Es. You know the media doesn't get too excited about Thanksgiving. They go from Halloween to Christmas . . . spooks to Santa. Maybe it is because Thanksgiving is something that happens in our homes and our hearts.

Es What do you mean?

J Like the warmth of a fire . . . families coming together; kids and grandkids . . . fussing around the kitchen . . . long distance phone calls . . . holding hands and praying together before that special meal . . .

Es The _____ vs. _____ *(insert names of teams playing on Thanksgiving)* and popcorn.

J You bet! Friends dropping by . . . pumpkin pie and homemade bread.

Es And ten million calories!

J And you know, Es, it's a day when we can remember all that God has done. God has provided all the important things of life.

Es Do you think one of our relatives had dinner with the Indians way back then?

J Well, I guess it's possible, but what we do know is that their gratefulness was passed down to us, and I hope we never lose that. Back then our forefathers needed each other to survive. And you know what, Es?

Es What?

J We still need each other . . . we need to stop on this day and be grateful for all those special people who make our lives better.

Es I'm thankful for my teacher . . . my church . . . *(turns to puppeteer)* . . . and you, Joannie.

J Thanks so much! Thanksgiving is a wonderful day, as it gives us a chance to be less selfish and more grateful . . . but do you know what I am REALLY grateful for . . . ?

Es What?

J Thursday . . . Thanksgiving Day is your day for dishes!

Es What? You gotta' be kidding!

J Kids, let's close with the THANK-YOU song you all know.

THANK YOU FOR THE WORLD SO SWEET

Thank you for the world so sweet,
Thank you for the food we eat,
Thank you for the birds that sing,
Thank you God for everything. Amen.

OR PRAYER:

Thank you for Thanksgiving! Help us to be thankful each and every day of the year. Amen.

J *(as kids are leaving)* Happy Thanksgiving everyone!

Es Hey, anyone good at doing dishes?

MEMORY MEMO
(MORE THAN A DRUMSTICK)

SONG
EXCITED—THANKSGIVING
   - America born
   - Alka Seltzer!
AUNT NANCY—Diet-Feed limit

NEW COUSIN—need worse
   - baby looks like Uncle Joe
   - Consideration

MEDIA
WARMTH OF FIRE— families coming together
   - kitchen
   - phone calls
   - pray
   - football games
   - friends
   - pie
   - bread
   - calories

ALL THE IMPORTANT THINGS
   OF LIFE

GRATEFULNESS—passed on

STILL NEED EACH OTHER

THANKFUL
   - teacher
   - church
   - you
   - less selfish
   - more grateful

DISHES

A BIRTHDAY CELEBRATION

IDEA: *Christmas*
PROPS: *Very large checked scarf around puppet's neck*

Es Knock knock.

J Who's there?

Es Dexter.

J Dexter who?

Es *(singing)* Dexter halls with boughs of holly . . .

J Fa . . . la . . . la . . . la . . . lalala.

Es Tis the season to be jolly . . .

J Fa . . . la . . . la . . . lalalala.

Es What's the matter . . . did ya forget the words?

J *(rather disgusted)* No, I didn't forget the words, Esmerelda . . . that's the way the song goes. Anyway, I've been looking at the scarf you're wearing today . . . I don't know how to say this, but isn't that pattern bit large for you?

Es Yeh, my rich aunt Sophie sent it to me.

J I see.

Es She asked me if I preferred a large check or a small check.

J Uh huh . . . and you said a large check.

Es Course, I didn't know she was talking about a scarf.

J Esmerelda . . .

Es *(interrupts)* Hey, Joannie. What happens when a cat walks in a sandbox on Christmas Day?

J Okay, Es, what does happen when a cat walks in a sandbox on Christmas Day?

Es It gets sandy claws. *(Santa Claus)*

J You are the cat's meow!

Es Yep, purrrrrrrfect in every way!

J You're sure in rare form today.
Es Guess I'm just trying to forget my awful day.

J Well, what day was that?

Es It was my birthday.

J Your birthday, and it was awful? I don't understand, Es . . . birthdays are supposed to be great.

Es Well, not this kid. I had the cupcakes all decorated, had lemonade, the decorations were super . . . all colors of balloons. I could hardly wait for my friends to arrive.

J I suppose they arrived with presents.

Es Well, sorta! When they put them on the table, I said, "Holy Cow, thanks guys!" Then Jenny said, "These aren't for you. Seeing as it's so close to Christmas we decided to have a gift exchange instead of the usual presents."

J No presents?

Es I guess not!

J Well, I bet they loved the decorations, all those colorful balloons and streamers.

Es Dan said they were nice, but he had a better idea. He took the balloons and tied one to each person's ankle, then everyone tried to stamp on the other person's balloon and break it . . . they hollered and had a great time.

J Gosh, Es *(sadly)* that took care of the decorations, didn't it? I know how you love games. What other games did you play?

Es Carla divided everyone into two groups, and we played Simon Says.

J I know you love that game.

Es I asked which group I was in, and Carla said, "It's your birthday, why don't you just watch," . . . like it was some stupid honor or something!

J Aw, Es, that is really awful.

Es Shucks! I felt terrible inside. It was like I wasn't even there! They didn't bring me any presents, or wish me "Happy Birthday." They took the decorations down and I couldn't even play my favorite game. I felt so lousy, Joannie.

J   They must've at least sung, "Happy Birthday."

Es   Well, Jan said something about saving her voice for the Christmas Concert and dingy Dorothy said, *(in wangy voice)* "I didn't come to this party just to sing some dumb Happy Birthday song."

J   Esmerelda, you really did have a disappointing day!

Es   Disappointing? Golly, Joannie, what good is a birthday when your friends don't even realize it's your special day?

J   I'm sorry, Esmerelda!

Es   I just sat in the corner and watched them playing and having a good time. *(very sadly)*I felt so lonely and left out, I felt like saying, "Hey, it's my Birthday!"

J   Es, I wish there was something I could do.

Es   *(slowly and thoughtfully said)* YOU KNOW JOANNIE . . . DO YOU THINK JESUS FEELS THIS WAY SOMETIMES? IT'S HIS BIRTHDAY . . . AND SO OFTEN HE ISN'T INCLUDED EITHER. *(Joannie looks at Esmerelda—a look exchanged as if to understand, maybe a nod of head—no words)*

J   Shall we pray:
Dear God:
Help us make this Christmas different. May we invite Jesus into our hearts and into our homes. Let us remember that this is His special day . . . His birthday! Amen.

MEMORY MEMO
(A BIRTHDAY CELEBRATION)

KNOCK-KNOCK
   Dexter

SCARF

HAPPENS—CAT WALK IN SANDBOX
   - Cat's meow

AWFUL DAY
   - Cupcakes
   - Lemonade
   - Decorations
   - Balloons

BALLOON ON ANKLE
SIMON SAYS

NO:
   - Presents
   - Didn't wish Happy Birthday
   - Took decor down
   - Favorite game

JAN—voice Christmas concert
DOROTHY—wangy

DISAPPOINTING DAY
   - lonely
   - left out

WONDER - JESUS FEELS THIS WAY

HIS BIRTHDAY—ISN'T INCLUDED EITHER

PRAYER

A POEM FOR THE SEASON

IDEA: *Christmas Season*
PROPS: *Puppet is dressed in a stocking cap and wrapped in a scarf*
Hint: *Easy to present—most of script is read*

J   My goodness, Esmerelda, you certainly are bundled up today.

Es   It's getting so cold out there . . . my teeth are still chattering.

J   I told you we were asked to read a poem about winter.

Es   Winter? Holy Cow, why did you pick winter?

J   Winter really is a wonderful time of year . . . fires in the fireplace . . . goodies baking . . . soup on the stove . . . skating . . . tobogganning. Do you like to toboggan?

Es   Sure. It always pays "to bargain" a little, you get a reduced price.

J   Really, Esmerelda, winter CAN be fun.

Es   You're kidding me, right? Snow, cold fingers, big heat bills, ice, why it's awful! *(Teeth still chattering)*

J   Why are you so negative today. People always complain about the weather. There seems to be as much complaining about the heat in the summer as there is about cold in the winter.

Es   That's true, we do complain about the heat, but there is one thing for sure . . . you don't have to shovel it!

J   You know something very interesting is that you can endure the cold for three hours while sledding, and only 3 minutes while shoveling.

Es   Well, it's this way . . . one has to do with enforced responsibility and one is my own choice.

J   C'mon, are you putting me on? You do like some things about winter, don't you?

Es   . . . *(long pause)*

J   Es . . .

Es   Yeah, I heard you. I'm trying to think . . . I guess I like the part about winter that deals with Santa and presents, candy, cookies, $10 from Uncle Willie!

J Esmerelda, do you only think of yourself? That isn't what makes the Christmas season.

Es Oh, now I know . . . *(begins singing)* Up on the housetop reindeer pause . . . here comes good old Santa Claus . . .

J Esmerelda . . . *(shakes head)* Uh-huh.

Es You mean I still don't got it?

J You still don't have it.

Es Boy, are you fussy!

J Well, anyway, let's read this poem. Do you want to help me read it?

Es Okay . . . *(figure nods head and looks at the paper)*

J Why don't you start . . .

Es *(Begins to read . . .)*

> 'Tis the season to be jolly!
> So the story goes,
> Why is it, then, that everybody
> Seems to have the woes?

J Could it be their hearts and minds,
Just cannot seem to find
The time to stop and focus
On the Savior of mankind?

Es For that's what Christmas is, you know.
The blessed, holy birth
Of God, the Father's only Son,
Who came to save the earth,

J From all this worry, rush and hassle,
That we seem to think a must.
When all our loved ones really want,
Is our friendship, love and trust.

Es So share the greatest gift of all,
Wrapped as a baby boy,
Who will never need replacing
Like a sweater, tie, or toy.

J   "Tis' the season to be jolly!"
Well, yes! But better, still,
Is the joy unspeakable in our hearts
That only Christ can fill!

by Alice Allen

Es   Oh, now I get it! That really makes winter the nicest part of the year, doesn't it? I take back all that bad stuff I said.

J   Yes, Esmerelda, to think a tiny baby could change the whole world . . . and turn winter into a bright wonderful season.

All Sing: Verse of "Away in the Manger" *to close.*

J   Thank you, God, for Christmas.

Es   Thank you, God, for Baby Jesus. Amen.

MEMORY MEMO
(A POEM FOR THE SEASON)

COLD—TEETH CHATTERING
- Winter—wonderful time
- fire—fireplace
- goodies baking
- soup on stove
- skating
- tobogganing "bargain"

CAN BE FUN—kidding
- snow
- cold fingers
- big heat bills
- ice

WHY SO NEGATIVE
- Heat—don't have to shovel it!
- Like about winter?
- Santa
- Presents
- Candy, cookies
- $10—Uncle Willie
- Sing: Up on Housetop

POEM: (read)

TINY BABY—change the whole world

WINTER—bright wonderful season

WHAT'S ADVENT?

<u>IDEA</u>: *Understanding Advent—1st Sunday in Advent*
<u>PROP</u>: *Christmas List (long)*

Es   *(Sings)* Deck the Halls with boughs of holly . . . fa . . . la . . . la . . . la . . . la . . . la, la . . . 'Tis the season to be jolly . . . fa . . . la . . . la . . . la . . . la la la.

J   What on earth are you doing?

Es Getting into the Christmas spirit . . . *(continues singing)*

J And what have you got there in your hand?

Es Well, these are just a few suggestions for Christmas. *(Vent looks at list which sticks about 3 inches below puppet's hand—puppeteer pulls out pin holding list and it falls to the floor.)*

J Esmerelda! This is awful. Don't you think this is a bit ridiculous? *(looking at list)* Let's see, I 'spose you have cookies, popcorn balls, and peanut brittle on here?

Es Cookies really taste great, but I want something that will last longer . . . food just doesn't last long after you've eaten it.

J That's true. *(looks at list)* A stereo?

Es Yeah, but I like it loud and you don't so that won't work.

J You are right there! *(looking at list again)* Precious Moments? Oh, yes, those cute faces . . . those little statues?

Es Yeah, but I've been thinking, they are expensive and get broken so easily.

J What about a swing? They are pretty hard to break.

Es No, they don't break, but you get too big for them after awhile.

J Scrabble would be fun, and you don't get too big for it.

Es I know, but I always get tired of playing the same old game. After I play it about ten times, I have it all figured out . . . then it isn't fun anymore.

J Well, Es, you could get clothes. Those are always nice.

Es I like new clothes. Maybe I'd like . . . no, they get stained, torn or worn out . . . if I don't grow out of them first. I want something that will last.

J Well, Es, while you are thinking about that, I want to tell you and all these kids, that today is the 1st Sunday in Advent.

Es Add Vents? You mean they are going to add vents . . . I think ONE ventriloquist around here is plenty!

J No, Esmerelda! Advent season begins today! You know the coming of Christmas.

Es Christmas! Oh, I just love Christmas! All those toys and candy and presents and food and toys and candy . . . *(continues thinking)* . . . what do I want?

154

J   Advent means preparing for Christmas, not just buying packages, decorating and baking, but anticipating Jesus' birthday.

Es   Did He have a huge birthday party? Birthdays! Oh, I just love birthdays. All those parties, and toys and candy and cake and toys and . . .

J   Stop! Esmerelda, stop! I can tell you like birthdays, but this birthday is different from all other birthdays. Even the guests were different. The guests that came to see the baby Jesus were animals in the stable, wisemen from the East, and shepherds with their flocks of sheep.

Es   SURE was a strange party!

J   But it was such a wonderful night, for you see Jesus was the Son of God.

Es   You mean Jesus was the Son of God, and he was born in a stable?

J   Jesus was so special that he was born in a tiny place as a tiny baby and grew up to be someone we try very hard to be like.

Es   You know, Joannie, if Jesus were here today I guess he wouldn't think about what he was going to get. I guess he would be more concerned about others.

J   I know he would, Es.

Es   I shouldn't care so much about me. Maybe I could help around the house 'cuz I know you are really busy.

J   *(surprised)* THAT IS REALLY NICE!

Es   I should be more patient with my sister, and I will go visit Gramma Hanson down the street, 'cuz she doesn't have any family left.

J   Esmerelda, I think you have it! Those are the kinds of gifts that won't break or wear out or get old. You make others happy and you know what . . . it really makes you happy.

Es   Does that mean we can't do all that Christmas stuff?

J   Of course not! Jesus wants us to have fun on his birthday. Santa, the presents, the songs . . . they are all a part of a big birthday party for Jesus. *(looks at kids)* What do you say we all sing Happy Birthday to Jesus? . . . Okay, kids, you all have to sing!

EVERYONE: *(Everyone sings Happy Birthday to Jesus)*

J   I guess that is what Advent is all about . . . getting ready for Jesus' birthday.

Es Happy Advent everyone . . . and Merry Christmas too!
(*Hums* "Deck the Halls")

PRAYER:
As we prepare for Jesus' birthday, may we keep him in our hearts. Amen.

MEMORY MEMO
(WHAT'S ADVENT?)

SINGS: Deck the Halls

GOT IN YOUR HAND?
- Suggestions for Christmas—(*pull out list*)
"awful—ridiculous"

COOKIES, POPCORN—doesn't last after eat

PRECIOUS MOMENTS—expensive, broken

SWING—too big after while

SCRABBLE—fun, get tired of playing it

CLOTHES—stained, torn, worn out

ADVENT: means preparing for Christmas—
anticipating Jesus' birthday
- Huge party—toys, candy, cake . . .

Stop! Different
- even guests different—Wisemen
Shepherds
- Strange party
- Jesus—Son of God
Born:
- Tiny place
- Tiny baby
- grew up to be someone we'd like to be like

JESUS—More concerned about others

Esmerelda
- Help around house
- Visit Gramma Hanson

THOSE KIND OF GIFTS WON'T BREAK

JESUS WANTS US TO HAVE FUN ON BIRTHDAY

SING: Happy Birthday to Jesus

SOME WARMTH FOR THE JENKINS FAMILY

<u>IDEA:</u> *Christmas—caring about others — A story re-told*
(*Esmerelda sings the following to the tune of "The Man on the Flying Trapeze*)

Es (*sings*) He flies through the air with the greatest of ease,
The jolly fat man in the Red B.V.D.'s.

J (*shocked . . . surprised*) What?

Es *(Es repeats verse)*
He flies through the air with the greatest of ease,
The jolly fat man in the Red B.V.D.'s.

J That's what I thought you said . . . where on earth did you learn that?

Es You just have to be observant and you pick up all kinds of good stuff!

J Have you decided what you are going to give your friend Lou for Christmas?

Es I really don't know.

J What did you give her last year?

Es The measles!

J Oh dear, how could I forget?

Es I sure hope I get some big presents this year.

J Esmerelda, it's not the size of the present that counts. It's the thought behind it.

Es Well, I hope they all THINK a little bigger this Christmas.

J You really do embarrass me sometimes, you know that? But I have a story I'd like to tell you.

Es Great! I love stories.

J Well, this happened quite a few years ago just before Christmas in Chicago. Chuck and his sister Agnes ran a heating company.

Es What did Agnes do?

J Well, she was the buyer, hirer, firer, phone answerer, typist, bookkeeper, office girl and coffee maker.

Es Wow, she sorta' ran the place.

J Agnes would bring sandwiches to a crew working in an icy basement at three in the morning, but she was a Hard Hearted Hannah when it came to spending any of the company's money.

Es You mean she was a Scrooge and a tightwad?

J You are DEFINITELY right there. One day about a week before Christmas, all the phones in the office seemed to start ringing at once. There were more broken boilers, burned-out firepots, stuck stack switches than ever before. The men were working around the clock.

Es Wow, I 'spose everyone wanted to be sure they had heat for Christmas.

J Right. Agnes was writing names down as fast as she could, when one woman called from a very poor neighborhood. She had called one heating company after another trying to find someone who would fix her broken heater.

Es They were really cold?

J Oh yes, but Agnes, being a business woman first, asked if she could pay her bill, and Mrs. Jenkins said she would try and pay a little each month, so Agnes said she would try and get a man there soon as possible.

Es I bet she was happy.

J She sure was, she said, "God Bless you, Miss." Then Agnes turned the call over to Chuck, as all the other men were out. "Bump that other call I gave you; they only have a noisy burner. This is a "no-heat." Better get right on it." Chuck left and was gone for several hours.

Es Did he get it fixed?

J Well, when he came back, he said to Agnes. "Forget the billing on that one." "Well," Agnes said, "since WHEN are we are in the charity business?"

Es Boy, she WAS an old Scrooge!

J Chuck told Agnes that Mrs. Jenkins was a widow with seven children. Her house was clean, but very bare, hardly any furniture. The children were thin and hungry, wearing patched clothes.

Es Maybe they would get new ones for Christmas.

J Chuck said, *(turning to Esmerelda)* when he got the heat started one of the smaller boys came over to watch, and Chuck asked the little boy, "What did you tell Santa Claus you wanted for Christmas?"

Es I bet he wanted _____ *(use name of popular toy)*.

J The child looked Chuck right in the eye and said, "Ain't no more Santa Claus. Mama says, no use to ask for any toys, 'cause he is dead."

Es *(surprised)* He said that? I feel so sad.

J Agnes never said a word, she just handed Chuck another call. They all

158

worked most of the night, and the next morning Agnes called into the office to say she would be late coming to work.

Es   Guess she was all tuckered out!

J   Chuck seemed really happy she wasn't coming in. He asked one of the men to watch the phones, and mumbled something like, "Can't spend a dime without that woman looking over my shoulder," and out the door he went.

Es   Where'd he go, Joannie?

J   He headed right for the toy store. He hummed and whistled as he loaded toys into the cart. Dolls, games, trucks, a space ship. He grabbed some candy canes and stocking . . .

Es   I bet I know where he is going!

J   He drove through the snow all the way to the West Side, unloaded the presents and rang Mrs. Jenkins' doorbell.

Es   *(excited)* What happened?

J   When Chuck walked in, the children were whooping and hollering and singing and laughing. They were so excited, and Mrs. Jenkins was smiling through her tears. As he set his packages down he looked up and guess what?

Es   What?

J   There was Agnes pinning a star on top of a beautiful Christmas Tree!

Es   You mean Hard Hearted Hannah! What did she say when she saw Chuck?

J   She said, "Well, don't just stand there, get busy!" She paused a minute . . . then said ". . . and what took you so long?"

Es   *(cocks her head)* Is that what you mean when you talk about keeping Jesus in Christmas?

J   It sure is, Es. When Jesus is in our heart, we really do care about others.

Es   I sure liked that story!

J   Esmerelda, let's close with that song you learned in Sunday School.

Es   Great, Joannie.

SING ANY FAVORITE CAROL *(Maybe the song could be played on the piano and Esmerelda sing it once followed by everyone singing together in closing)*

Suggestions: *Children of the Heavenly Father*

MEMORY MEMO
(SOME WARMTH FOR THE JENKINS FAMILY)

SING: He flies thru the air . . .

Give friend Lou—last year measles

STORY: Heating Co. Chuck, sister Agnes
- Agnes—buyer, hirer, phone, typist, bookkeeper, office girl, coffee maker
  - sandwiches crew
  - Hard-hearted Hannah—money
- Near Christmas—phones ringing
- One woman—poor neighborhood
- pay—bit each month
- Bump call—only noisy burner—this "no-heat"
- Chuck—"Forget bill on that one"
- Scrooge

MRS. JENKINS
- Widow—seven children
- house: clean—bare—hardly any furniture
- children: thin—hungry—patched clothes
- Chuck asked: What want—Christmas
  Mama says Santa dead
  - Agnes handed Chuck another call
  - Agnes called office—late
  - Chuck happy—"Can't spend dime with her looking over my shoulder"
- Drove to Mrs. Jenkins
- Got there—children whooping, hollering, singing
- Mrs. Jenkins smiling—tears

GUESS WHAT?
- There was Agnes— star on tree
- Hard-hearted Hannah
- "Well, don't just stand there, get busy . . . what took you so long?"

KEEPING JESUS IN CHRISTMAS

WHEN JESUS IN OUR HEART—CARE ABOUT OTHERS

ESMERELDA'S EGO

IDEA: *Christmas—Esmerelda—self-centered*
PROPS: *Santa hat and beard for Esmerelda (optional)*
Hint: *See ending footnote for follow-up activity*
(Puppet is dressed in white beard and red stocking cap and is singing to self)

Es I wish ME a Merry Christmas . . . I wish ME a Merry Christmas . . .

J What's all this ME stuff?

Es Well, I'm getting geared up to have the best Christmas ever. I want MYSELF to have a grrrrrrrrrrrreat Christmas!

J *(Shakes head in disgust)* Esmerelda! Christmas is a time of giving to others.

Es I've been wrapping presents for ME. Are they ever super. I'm a good shopper . . . however there is nothing like Christmas to put a little bounce in your checks!

J You've got that right!

Es I also have to send Christmas cards to my fan club.

J Fan Club! Isn't this a bit much? We should've named this script Esmerelda's Ego. *(or name to fit your puppet)* You know it is taking all my will-power to keep from telling you what I think in front of all these people. *(kids)*

Es If you said what you thought, you'd be speechless!

J What are you trying to do, make Me look like a DUMMY?

Es Well, I don't see why I should take all the credit!

J *(look of "I can't believe this," changes subject)* Well, sounds like you won't need much. I was sorta' wondering what I should give you for Christmas.

Es I don't want you to go out and buy me something like a lot of toys this year. I'd rather you just give me something you've made yourself.

J *(looks puzzled)* Like what?

Es MONEY!

J *(exasperated)* Esmerelda! The whole idea of Christmas is that God shared his greatest gift with us, by sending his son Jesus, and we in turn share

161

with others.

Es But who will give to me if I give to others?

J *(still frustrated)* You know, Es, I've always given to those I love, and there are always presents for me under the tree. I've never been disappointed.

Es Are you putting me one? Ummmmmmmmmmmm . . . buying for others and there will be presents for me? Doesn't make sense. *(At this point puppeteer slips into another puppet and sets Alvia beside or on lap—so puppet on each hand. Esmerelda could be humming Christmas tune while you are doing this.)*

Es *(singing)* I wish ME a Merry Christmas . . .

J Es, look who's here.

Es Alvia, hey, what are you giving yourself for Christmas?

ALVIA: What? Myself? Esmerelda, you don't give to yourself at Christmas.

Es I figured I better cover the bases.

ALVIA: YOUR bases? Kinda' reminds me of last year's Christmas pageant when you were the donkey.

Es What?

ALVIA: Weren't you the donkey last Christmas?

Es Well . . . they just didn't realize how much talent I had. I should've been the lead.

ALVIA: I've never seen a donkey like that before . . . never!

Es What's that 'spose to mean?

ALVIA: A donkey with a gold rope around its neck and a gold and silver blanket on its back . . . gimme a break! It had to be you.

Es My fan club suggested it. Anyway, that donkey needed a little sprucing up.

ALVIA: Honestly, Esmerelda, this is enough to make one sick!

J Say, you two . . . *(turns toward Esmerelda)* What Alvia is trying to say is that there is so much joy and excitement in giving to others, that you are missing something very special. Just how exciting will it be to open all those gifts you wrapped for yourself?

Es *(slowly)* Not much, Joannie. I know everything that is in there . . . no surprises.

ALVIA: I get so excited when I think of something nice to give to my mom or dad, or my brothers. I can hardly wait until my mom opens my present.

Es *(curious)* What did you get her?

ALVIA: Well, this year I covered a box with pretty paper and inside I have all these slips of paper . . . with promises to my mom.

Es Like what?

ALVIA: Well, one says: make my bed, or walk the dog, or clean the entry, or set the table. I know my mom will like that better than anything. She gets really tired sometimes.

Es That's cool. I guess I had Christmas figured all wrong. I need to think of others and forget about myself . . . I've been pretty selfish. I guess I didn't use very good judgment . . . *(turns to Joannie)* Where do you get good judgment?

J Well . . . Es, I guess good judgment comes from experience.

Es Then where does experience come from?

J Well . . . I'd have to say experience comes from *(pause)* . . . bad judgment.

ALVIA: Wow, Esmerelda. You should be a highly experienced individual!

Es I'll let that pass if you'll show me how to make one of those promise boxes for my mom.

ALVIA: Sure.

Es Now that I've turned things around a bit and got my priorities in order . . . does it mean I have to give up my fan club?

ALVIA: I really don't think SHE'LL mind.

Es Great, let's go . . . I want to get started . . . *(stops short)* SHE . . . Holy Cow, what's that 'spose to mean?

J Shall we pray:
Dear God,
We are so thankful for your gift of love at Christmastime . . . Baby Jesus. May we remember to give love this Christmas, because that is the most important gift of all. Amen.

Footnote: If there is time during this script *(if done in Sunday School)* have children list other ideas that might be put in the

MEMORY MEMO
(ESMERELDA'S EGO)

SINGS: I wish ME a Merry Christmas . . .
- Wrap presents for ME
- Christmas—bounce in checks
- Christmas cards—Fan Club
- Esmerelda' Ego
- Wants—some made self
- MONEY!

IDEA CHRISTMAS—God shared
                greatest gift
- "Who give me"
- Never disappointed

ANOTHER PUPPET
- Don't give to self
- Christmas pageant
- Donkey
    - gold rope
    - gold & silver blanket
    - Fan club suggested it
    - Donkey needed sprucing up

JOY, EXCITEMENT GIVING TO OTHERS
- Missing something special
- no surprises

OTHER PUPPET
- Excited when give something nice
- Promise box—mom

CHRISTMAS FIGURED WRONG
- Selfish
- Good judgment—where get?
    - experience
    - bad judgment
- Make promise box

GIVE UP FAN CLUB—Don't think
    SHE'LL mind

BECOME AS LITTLE CHILDREN

<u>IDEA</u>: *Christmas—Adults can learn from children*

Es *(Sing)* I wish you a Merry Christmas . . . I wish you a Merry Christmas . . . I wish you a Merry Christmas . . . and a . . . *(Notices audience)* Opppppppppps!

J That sounds nice to wish all these kids a Merry Christmas. Es! You told me you were reading Dickens. Do you know who Scrooge is?

Es No, who's he?

J He's the one who at Christmas said, "Bah-humbug!"

Es Oh . . . I thought that was the mailman! *(looks around)*

J Es, what are you looking for?

Es My book . . . it's here somewhere. *(continues looking)* Joannie, I guess I can't find my book, but could you tell me the Christmas story?

J   Well, sure . . . Once upon a time there lived a fat, jolly old man with a long white beard and a big red bag fill . . .

Es   No, Joannie, the one that's in my book . . . (*looks around again*) Maybe I left it in Sunday school.

J   Which book, Esmerelda?

Es   It's my Bible and the story's about baby Jesus.

J   (*bit embarrassed, clears throat*) Oh . . . well . . . ah . . .

Es   You know the story, don't you, Joannie?

J   Why . . . ah . . . of course I do.

Es   Well, then, tell it to me. I want to hear it.

J   Okay. A long time ago in a far off country . . .

Es   How far?

J   A long way . . .

Es   Past California?

J   Yes, a long ways. It was in Bethlehem.

Es   Bethlehem? Where's that? Is it past Florida?

J   Yes, way past Florida. Mary and Joseph were on a trip and Mary was going to have a baby, so she was very tired when they arrived. Joseph went to many inns, but there wasn't any room anywhere.

Es   That's awful! Did they try the Super 8 or Motel 6?

J   Well, they didn't have those kind of inns then, and Joseph was getting worried as it got later and later.

Es   Didn't he have a Visa of master Card? You can get anything with one of those!

J   No, he was very poor, Esmerelda.

Es   I guess that's why they traveled on a donkey instead of a Ford Bronco, huh?

J   (*laughs a bit*) Esmerelda, don't confuse Bible times with today. Well, finally one innkeeper told Joseph that he could use the barn behind the inn. So Mary and Joseph took shelter there with the cows, sheep and donkeys. That night Jesus was born. Mary wrapped him in a blanket and laid him in a manger, because there was no room for them in the inn. A manger is a place where hay is put to feed the cattle.

Es You mean they laid him in a cow's dinner plate?

J Cow's dinner plate! Well, that's an interesting way to put it, but yes, and that stable became a place where a miracle was born.

Es But if Jesus was the Son of God, why didn't he get born in a circus or the Super Dome or something like that?

J Isn't it something, Es, that a small baby could be born in a crude stable and grow up to be the Son of God. He was God's gift to us.

Es A gift?

J Yes, God wanted us to know how to live so he sent Jesus to show us how we should love each other.

Es *(Puppet looks at Puppeteer)* I guess God must be real disappointed sometimes, huh, Joannie? What's the matter, Joannie, you look so sad.

J Es, I guess I was just thinking about the Shepherds and the Wisemen, the angels that sang their praises on that beautiful night so many years ago. Thank you so much, Esmerelda, for making me see something so important.

Es I did?

J Yes, you opened my eyes. I think we've gotten away from some really important things in this family and I'm going to change them . . . now.

Es What do you mean?

J I mean that Christmas is Jesus' birthday! I've gotten so hung up with things to do, what to buy, what to feed everyone . . . *(pause)* but things will be different now.

Es *(thoughtfully)* I guess what we need to do is take baby Jesus out of the manger and hold him in our hearts.

J I really like that Esmerelda . . . take him out of the manger and hold him in our hearts. Let's do it!

Es *(whispers in Joannie's ear)*

J Esmerelda would like us all to sing together, *"Come into my Heart Lord Jesus."*

166

Prayer: Sing together or Esmerelda could sing a verse, then kids.

Into my Heart, Into my heart,
Come into my heart, Lord Jesus
Come in today, come in to stay,
Come into my heart, Lord Jesus

MEMORY MEMO
(BECOME AS LITTLE CHILDREN)

SING: I wish you a Merry Christmas . . .
- Deck the halls
- read Dickens
- Scrooge

WHERE'S MY BOOK . . .
- Christmas story—"fat, jolly, old man . . ."
- "no . . . in Bible . . . baby Jesus"

STORY:
- Far country—"how far"—past Florida
- No room inn—Super 8, Motel 6
- Visa—Master Card
- Donkey—Ford Bronco
- use barn—Jesus born—manger—feed cattle
- Cow's dinner plate
- why born circus, Super Dome?
- Sent Jesus to show us how to love one another
- Sad—thinking of Shepherds, Wisemen, Angels
- Thank you—making me see
- Gotten away from important things—change—hung up—to do, to buy, to feed

**NEED TO TAKE BABY JESUS OUT OF THE MANGER
AND HOLD HIM IN OUR HEARTS.**

SING: Come into my Heart Lord Jesus

ADDITIONAL RIDDLES AND HUMOR

<u>GENERAL</u>

1. With what two animals do you always go to bed?
    (Calves)

2. Which eats more grass, black sheep or white sheep?
    (White—more of them)

3. What is the difference between a donkey and a postage stamp?
    (One you lick with a stick, other you stick with a lick)

4. To what man do men always take their hats off?
    (The barber)

5. When the clock strikes 13, what time is it?
    (Time to get the clock fixed)

6. What question can never be answered by "YES?"
    (Are you asleep?)

7. When will water stop running down hill?
    (When it reaches the bottom)

8. What is the smallest bridge in the world?
    (Bridge of your nose)

9. Why do we look over a stone wall?
    (Because we can't see thru it)

10. Why is your hand like a hardware store?
    (It has nails)

11. What is it that has four legs and only one foot?
    (Bed)

12. What is bought by the yard and worn by the foot?
    (Carpet)

13. Why did the jelly roll?
    (It saw the apple turn-over)

14. Why is your nose not 12 inches long?
    (Because it would then be a foot)

15. When are cooks cruel?
    (When they beat the eggs and whip the cream)

16. How far can you go into the woods?
    (As far as the center, then you'll be going out)

17. Why is a hen sitting on a fence like a nickel?
    (Because she has a head on one side and a tail on the other)

18. What is full of holes, yet holds water?
    (Sponge)

19. Why is a quarrel like dancing?
    (It takes two)

20. What does everyone give and few take?
    (Advice)

21. What is it that is so brittle that even to name it is to break it?
    (Silence)

22. When is a black dog not a black dog?
    (When he's a greyhound)

23. What KEY is the hardest to turn?
    (DonKEY)

24. What is yours and used by others more than yourself?
    (Your name)

25. What goes up and never goes down?
    (Your age)

26. What has four wheels and flies?
    (A garbage truck)

27. When is a boy like a pony?
    (When he's a little hoarse)

28. What bird is very rude?
    (Mockingbird)

29. What goes uphill and downhill and stays in the same place?
    (Road)

30. The more you take away the larger it grows? What is it?
    (A hole)

31. What is the difference between an Elephant and a Flea?
    (An elephant can have fleas, but fleas can't have elephants.)

32. What room can no one enter?
    (A mushroom)

33. In what kind of cord is it impossible to tie a knot?
    (Cord of wood)

34. What driver never gets arrested?
    (A Screw driver)

35. How did Thomas Edison feel when he invented the light bulb?
    (Mr. Edison was delighted)

36. What tune makes everyone glad?
    (Fortune)

37. What does an artist like to draw best?
    (His salary)

38. Why is the sun like a good loaf of bread?
    (Because it's light when it rises)

39. Why should potatoes grow better than other vegetables?
    (Because they have eyes to see what they are doing)

40. What is the difference between a hungry man and a glutton?
    (One longs to eat, the other eats too long)

41. Why is an old man like a window?
    (He's full of panes [pains])

42. What asks no questions, but requires many answers?
    (A Doorbell)

43. When do elephants have eight feet?
    (When there are two of them)

44. Styles change, but what can a person wear that is never out of style?
    (A smile)

45. When is an ear of corn like a question?
    (When you're popping it)

46. Why did the tomato blush?
   (It saw the salad dressing)

47. Who always goes to bed with his shoes on?
   (The horse)

48. What question is that to which you positively must answer yes?
   (What does y-e-s spell?)

49. Why is an empty purse always the same?
   (There is never any change in it)

50. When is music like vegetables?
   (Four [beats] beets to the measure)

51. Why is a trap like the measles?
   (It's catching)

52. What is there in your house that ought to be looked into?
   (A mirror)

53. What is the highest public building in your city?
   (Library—has the most stories)

54. What is the difference between a new nickel and an old dime?
   (5 cents)

55. What is that which every living person has seen, but will never see again?
   (Yesterday)

56. What would happen if a girl swallowed her spoon?
   (She couldn't stir)

57. What is that which never uses its teeth for eating purposes?
   (Comb)

58. What table doesn't have a leg to stand on?
   (Multiplication Table)

59. When is it okay to lie?
   (In bed)

60. What roof never keeps out the wet?
   (Roof of the mouth)

61. What is that which is put on the table, and cut, but never eaten?
   (A deck of cards)

62. What is always behind time?
    (The back of a clock)

63. What kind of ears does an engine have?
    (Engineers)

64. What has a mouth, but never eats?
    (River)

65. What is the last thing you take before going to bed?
    (You feet off the floor)

66. When is it that your jacket pocket is empty, but still has something in it?
    (When it has a hole in it)

67. When was beef the highest that it has ever been?
    (When the cow jumped over the moon)

68. Which is the largest room in the world?
    (Room for improvement)

69. Why should an artist never be short of cash?
    (He can always draw money)

70. Where does Thursday come before Wednesday?
    (In the Dictionary)

71. What is the difference between a ballet dancer and a duck?
    (One is quick on her feet; the other quack on her feet)

72. When is a boat like a pile of snow?
    (When it's adrift)

73. What has eyes, but cannot see?
    (Potatoes)

74. What is the surest way to double your money?
    (Fold it)

75. What is it that once it's lost you can never find it again?
    (Time)

76. Why is a colt like an egg?
    (It must be broken before used)

77. What is the difference between a woman and a postage stamp?
    (One is female; the other mail-fee)

78. Why is a ship the most polite thing in the world?
(Goes forward with a bow)

79. When is a river like the letter "T"?
(When it's crossed)

80. What is the best thing to put into a hamburger?
(Your teeth)

81. What smells the most in a bakery?
(Your nose)

82. Why can't the world ever come to an end?
(It's round)

83. What do ants put under their arms?
(Ant-iperspirant)

84. Where can happiness always be found?
(In the dictionary)

85. Name something that can sing and has eight legs?
(A quartet)

86. Why does a person who is sick lose his sense of touch?
(He does not feel well)

87. If you see a man scratching his head, what time is it?
(Five after one)

88. What most resembles a half an orange?
(the other half)

89. When is an apple awful?
(When it's a crab)

90. What is the difference between a watchmaker and a jailer?
(One sells watches; the other watches cells)

91. What is it that has a face, but no head, hand, but no feet; yet travels everywhere and is usually running?
(A watch)

92. What is a well-dressed lion called?
(A dandelion)

93. What is it that a person can place in his right hand which cannot be placed in his left hand?   *(His elbow)*

173

94. Which is bigger, Mr. Bigger or Mr. Bigger's baby?
     (The baby is a little bigger)

95. Which is the strongest day of the week?
     (Sunday—the rest are week [weak] days)

96. What is the difference between an organist and his cold?
     (One knows his stops; the other stops his nose)

97. What goes through a door but never goes in or comes out?
     (A Keyhole)

98. What is the difference between a pound of lead and a pianist?
     (Lead weighs a pound and pianist pounds away)

99. What does a tree have that a tooth has?
     (Roots)

100. What bird do you think can lift the heaviest weights?
     (Crane)

101. What is it that cannot run even though it has three feet?
     (A yardstick)

102. What is the difference between a sewing machine and a kiss?
     (One sews seams so nice; the other seems so nice)

103. What increases its value one-half when turned upside down?
     (#6)

104. I'll tell you something that will tickle you. What?
     (A feather)

105. What is the difference between a cat and a match?
     (A cat lights on its feet; a match lights on its head)

106. What's worse than raining cats and dogs?
     (Hailing a cab)

107. What has a bed, but never sleeps?
     (A River)

108. What did Paul Revere say when finishing his famous ride?
     (Whoa)

109. On which side does a chicken have the most feathers?
     (the outside)

110. When is a blue book not a blue book?
(When it's read [red])

111. What speaks every language?
(An echo)

112. In what line of work do you always find things dull?
(One who sharpens knives or scissors)

113. Why is a racehorse like a leaky milk carton?
(It runs)

114. Which pine has the longest needles?
(Porcupine)

115. What is it you cannot see, but is always before you?
(Your future)

116. What is the best way to turn people's heads?
(Go to church late)

117. Why does a dog turn around three times before lying down?
(One good turn deserves another)

118. What's all over the house?
(The roof)

119. Why does time fly?
(Because so many people are trying to kill it)

120. What is the difference between a tight shoe and an oak tree?
(One makes corns ache, the other makes a-corns)

121. What two letters of the alphabet contain nothing?
(M and T [empty])

122. What word is always pronounced wrong?
(Wrong)

123. When is coffee like the soil?
(When it's ground)

124. When are houses like books?
(When they have stories)

125. Why do you always put on your left shoe last?
(Because when you put on one, the other is left)

126. When is an altered dress like a secret?
(When it's let out)

127. Why is a wedding band like the sound of a bell?
(It's a ring)

128. Why does a cat wag its tail?
(Because it wants to)

129. What nation always wins in the end?
(Determination)

130. What is the best thing to take when one is run down?
(The number of the car)

131. What is hard to beat?
(A drum with a hole in it)

132. What age is served for breakfast?
(Sausage)

133. What are the most difficult ships to conquer?
(Hardships)

134. What four letters would scare a robber or thief?
(O I C U)

135. Which is proper to say, 5 plus 4 IS 11 or ARE 11?
(Neither; 5 plus 4 = 9)

136. Why does a dog bite his tail?
(To make both ends meet)

137. What has six feet and can sing?
(A trio)

138. What part of the fish weighs the most?
(Scales)

139. Why are fish so well educated?
(They are found in schools)

140. When is a pig like ink?
(When you put it in a pen)

141. What bird is depressed?
(Bluebird)

142. Why is a goose like an icicle?
    (*They both grow down*)

143. What is the hardest thing about learning to ride a bicycle?
    (*The sidewalk*)

144. What has no head, or arms, or legs, and still has a tongue and a toe?
    (*A shoe*)

145. What is the difference between 1941 and 1949 model automobiles?
    (*8 years*)

146. What birds have four feet and yellow feathers?
    (*Two canaries*)

147. Why did John's mother send him three socks when he was in college?
    (*Because he wrote he'd grown so tall—he'd grown another foot*)

148. What is the surest way to keep water from coming into your house?
    (*Don't pay your water bill*)

149. Which is heavier, a pound of lead or a pound of feathers?
    (*Each weighs a pound*)

150. Why are different trees like different dogs?
    (*Each has a different bark*)

151. What is the difference between a well-dressed man and a tired dog?
    (*Man wears an entire suit and dog just pants*)

152. What is it that looks like a cat, eats like a cat, walks like a cat, yet is not a cat?
    (*a kitten*)

153. What is that which you can keep even after giving it to someone else?
    (*Your word*)

154. What is the difference between an engineer and a school teacher?
    (*One minds the train—the other trains the mind*)

155. Why is a man in jail like a boat full of water?
    (*Both need bailing out*)

156. What is that which has never been felt, seen or heard, never existed and still has a name?
    (*Nothing*)

157. What is the difference between a farmer and a dressmaker?
(One gathers what he sows; the other sews what she gathers)

158. If a man gets up on a horse, where should he get down?
(From a goose)

159. Why is a room full of married folks like an empty room?
(Because there isn't a single person in it)

160. What is the difference between a soldier and a girl?
(One faces the powder; the other powders her face)

161. When is a brown dog most likely to enter a house?
(When the door is open)

162. Why is a thief comfortable?
(Because he takes things easy)

163. What fish is most valued by a bride?
(Her-ring)

164. What is it that can play but can't walk?
(Piano)

165. What continent do you see when you look in the mirror in the morning?
(Europe—"you're up")

166. Why is a pig in the house like a house on fire?
(The sooner it's put out the better)

167. What is it that has neither skin, bone or nail and yet has four fingers and a thumb?
(A glove)

168. What insect is found in school?
(Spelling bee)

169. Why is a dog's tail like the center of a tree?
(Because it's farthest from the bark)

170. What makes more noise than a pig in a pen?
(Two pigs)

171. What animal keeps the best time?
(Watch dog)

172. What is the most moral instrument?
(Upright piano)

173. What is the hardest thing to deal with?
(An old deck of cards)

174. What ship has two mates but no captain?
(Courtship)

175. What is it that runs in and out of town all day and night?
(Road)

176. What is the difference between one yard and two yards?
(A fence)

177. What coat is finished without buttons and put on wet?
(A coat of paint)

178. What well-known band never plays popular music?
(Head-band)

179. What is the difference between the sun and bread?
(The sun rises in the east; bread rises with yeast)

180. If two's company, and three's a crowd, what are four and five?
(Nine)

181. What is the difference between a cat and a comma?
(The cat has claws at the end of his paws; the comma is a pause at the end of a clause.)

182. Why should you never tell secrets in a cornfield?
(Too many ears and they would be shocked)

183. What is the best way to carry water in a sieve?
(Freeze it first)

184. What are the biggest kind of ants?
(gi-ants)

185. What should a minister preach about?
(about 5 minutes)

186. Which are the most sensible letters?
(The Y's—"wise")

187. When should a pig be able to write?
(When he's turned into a pen)

188. What do you call a man who is always wiring for money?
(An electrician)

189. Why does a silver car never pay toll?
(Because the driver pays it)

190. Why did Humpty Dumpty have a great fall?
(To make up for a terrible summer)

191. What's worse than a giraffe with a sore throat?
(A hippopotamus with chapped lips)

192. What is the best way to keep fish from smelling?
(Cut off their noses)

193. What do you call a camel without a hump?
(Humphrey)

194. What do you get when you cross an elephant with a computer?
(A 5,000 pound know-it-all)

195. What is the difference between unlawful and illegal?
(Illegal is a sick bird)

196. What did one candle say to the other candle?
(Are you going out tonight?)

197. There are ten cats in a boat. One jumped out. How many are left?
(None, they were all copycats)

198. What did the kid say when he lost his dog?
(Doggone)

199. What tree is known for clapping?
(Palm tree)

200. Why was the lady's hair mad?
(Because she teased it)

201. Why should bowling alleys be quiet?
(So that you can hear a pin drop)

202. Why did Meg go outside with her purse open?
(She expected some change in the weather)

203. What did Bugs Bunny say to the light bulb?
(Watts up, Doc?)

204. What did one firefly say to the other firefly?
(Your son sure is bright for his age)

205. What did one mountain say to the other after the earthquake?
(It wasn't my fault)

206. Did you hear about the frog that double parked?
(It got toad "towed")

207. Why doesn't a motorcycle stand up by itself?
(Because it's two-tired)

207. What kind of sharks never eat women?
(Man-eating sharks)

208. Why did the astronaut stop writing in his journal?
(Because he was outer space)

209. What did the big chimney say to the little chimney?
(You're too young to smoke)

210. What is a cat's favorite color?
(Purrrrrrple)

211. What do you call a vacuum race?
(A Kirby Derby)

212. Which animal is the strongest?
(Snail—he carries his house)

213. What can't you eat for breakfast?
(Lunch and dinner)

214. Why do cows wear bells?
(Because their horns don't work)

215. Who invented spaghetti?
(Someone who used his noodle)

216. What do you get if you cross a centipede with a parrot?
(A walkie talkie)

217. What did the digital clock say to its mother?
(Look, Ma, no hands)

218. What is the best way to see flying saucers?
(Trip the waitress)

219. What did the mayonnaise say to the refrigerator?
    (Shut the door, I'm dressing)

220. Why did the girl sit on the watch?
    (She wanted to be on time)

221. Where do pencils live?
    (Pencil-vania)

222. What kind of books do you read on a boat?
    (Ferry tales)

223. What do you call a boring bird at the seashore?
    (A dull gull)

224. Why didn't the tree play checkers?
    (Because it was a chess nut)

225. Elmer: Do you have any idea why Mr. Grossowochikiowski would want to change his name?
    Peter: Well, it's hard to say . . .

226. Why did the dog go to court?
    (He got a barking ticket)

227. Why did the bird put a desk in her tree?
    (She was opening a branch office)

228. Why don't statues laugh?
    (Because they'll crack up)

229. Why did the soldier salute the refrigerator?
    (Because it was a General Electric)

230. What did the farmer say to the disappointed cow?
    (Sorry, I gave you a bum steer)

231. What do you call a cat that eats lemons?
    (A sourpuss)

232. What is red and goes up and down, up and down?
    (A tomato in an elevator)

233. What did the limestone say to the geologist?
    (Stop taking me for granite)

234. What did the bread say to the other bread?
    (You're looking crummy today!)

SEASONAL

SPRING
1.   What flower does a person carry around all year?
     (Tulips)

2.   What two flowers should be at the zoo?
     (The Dandelion and the Tiger Lily)

3.   Five kids were under an umbrella and none of them got wet. How did
     they do it?
     (It wasn't raining)

4.   If a farmer can raise 250 bushels in dry weather, what does he raise in
     wet weather?
     (Umbrella)

5.   Why do ducks and geese fly North in Springtime? or South in Fall?
     (It's too far to walk)

6.   Why is early grass like a pen-knife?
     (Spring brings out the blades)

7.   (APRIL) Why should soldiers be tired on the first of April?
     (They've just gone through a March of 31 days)

8.   Why is a tired man like an umbrella?
     (He is used up)

9.   SPRING-SUMMER—How does a garden laugh?
     (Hoe, Hoe, Hoe)

10. What does a person usually grow in a garden if he works hard?
     (Tired)

SUMMER
1.   Where does a sick boat go?
     (To the doc "dock")
2.   What kind of sport does a mosquito like?
     (Skin diving)

3.   What did one strawberry say to the other?
     (If you had listened to me, we wouldn't be in this jam!)

WINTER
1.   Which travels faster, heat or cold?
     (Heat—You catch cold)

183

2. Why is snow different from Sunday?
    (It can fall on any day of the week)

SPECIAL DAYS OR MONTHS

JANUARY
* What is the difference between a U.S. President and an old hat?
(One is sworn in, the other worn out)

* Why is a good resolution like a mirror?
(It's easily broken)

FEBRUARY
* What American has had the largest family?
(George Washington—Father of our Country)

* In what month do girls talk the least?
(Feb. it's the shortest)

* Why was Washington buried standing?
(Because he couldn't lie)

JULY
* What did the big firecracker say to the little firecracker?
(My pop's bigger than your pop!)

* Why is the emblem of the United States more enduring than that of France, England, Ireland or Scotland?
The "Lily" may fade and its leaves decay,
The "Rose" from its stem may sever,
The "Shamrock" and "Thistle" may pass away,
But the "Stars" will shine forever.

OCTOBER
* What instrument does the skeleton play?
(Trombone)

* What does Count Dracula do at 10:30?
(He takes a coffin-break)

* What does a ghost keep in the barn stall?
(A night mare)

* Why did the skeleton cross the road?
(To get to the body shop)

* Where does a ghost go for a swim?
(At the Dead Sea)

NOVEMBER
* What is the best KEY to a good dinner?
(TurKEY)

* Why does Uncle Sam wear red, white and blue suspenders?
(To hold up his pants)

* Which president wore the largest hat?
(The one with the biggest head)

* Why are lobsters like many politicians?
(They change color when they get in hot water)

DECEMBER
* On what toe does corn never come?
(Mistletoe)

* What is filled every morning and emptied every night except once a year when it is filled at night and emptied in the morning?
(A stocking)

* Why is the letter R important to us kids?
(Because without it there wouldn't be Christmas or New Year's)

* What do we have in December that we do not have in any other month?
(The letter D)

* What happens to a cat when it walks in a sand box on Christmas Day?
(It gets sandy claws [Santa Claus])

* Why do children object to the absence of Santa Claus?
(They prefer his presence "presents")

* What did the frog say on Christmas?
(Hoppy holiday)

WEATHER

1. When is the worst weather for rats and mice?
   (When it rains cats and dogs)

2. When are you in a country in South America?
   (When you are CHILI)

3. What falls often and never gets hurt?
   (Snow)

4. Why can't it rain for two days straight?
   (Because there is a night in between)

5. What contains more feet in winter than in summer?
   (Outdoor skating rink)

6. Knock, Knock
   (Who's there
   Snow
   Snow who
   Snow use talking to you)

BIBLE

1. What animal took the most luggage into the Ark?
   (Elephant—took his trunk)

2. Who was the greatest actor in the Bible?
   (Sampson—he brought the house down)

3. How did Jonah feel when the whale swallowed him?
   (Down in the mouth)

4. Who was the straightest man in the Bible?
   (Joseph, because Pharaoh made a ruler out of him.)

5. Why couldn't they play cards on the ark?
   (Because Noah sat on the deck)

6. What man in the Bible was the busiest doctor?
   (Job—he had more patients [patience] than any man)

7. Where was Solomon's temple?
   (on the side of his head)

8. When was pork first introduced into the Navy?
   (When Noah brought Ham into the Ark)

9. How long did Cain hate his brother?
   (As long as he was Abel)

10. What time of the day was Adam created?
    (Just a little before Eve)

11. If a white stone fell into the Red Sea, what would happen?
    (It would get wet)

12. When was tennis mentioned in the Bible?
    (When Joseph served in Pharaoh's court)

13. Who first introduced walking sticks?
    (Eve—when she presented Adam with a little Cain [cane])

14. Why was Adam's first day the longest?
    (Because it had no Eve)

15. What was Noah's favorite country record?
    ("I Love a Rainy Night")

16. What is that which Adam never had, yet gave two to each of his children?
    (Parents)

17. How do we know they had fruit on board the Ark?
    (Animals went in pairs—"pears")

18. When was the first automobile breakdown in the Bible?
    (When Moses threw a rod)

19. What kind of lights did Noah's ark have?
    (Floodlights)

20. Eve was the first person who ate herself out of house and home.

21. I wonder how many fig leaves Eve tried on before she said, "I'll take this one."

22. Who was the fastest runner in the world?
    (Adam, because he was first in the human race)

23. What simple affliction brought about the death of Sampson?
    (Fallen arches)

24. One thing about Noah, he sure didn't miss the boat.

25. Why was Solomon the wisest man in the world?
    (Because he had so many wives to advise him.)

26. What animal took the most luggage into the ark?
    (The elephant, he took his trunk, while the fox took a brush and the rooster took a comb)

27. When was baseball mentioned in the Bible?
    (When Rebecca walked to the well with the pitcher)

28. What advice did Noah give his sons about fishing off the ark?
    (Go easy boys, we only have two worms)

CHURCH

1. What do you call a non-church goer?
   (A Seventh-Day Absentist)

2. Did you hear about the dead angel?
   (He died of harp failure)

3. What is a minister doing when he rehearses his sermon?
   (Practicing what he preaches)

4. One should not fear flying. The Bible says, "I am with you always."

5. Minister: If absence makes the heart grow fonder, a lot of people must love our church.

6. It's more blessed to give than to receive. Beside, you don't have to write thank-you notes.

7. Many people treat their religion like a spare tire; they only use it in an emergency.

7. What is a prime minister?
   (A prime minister is a preacher at his best)

SPORTS

1. What has eighteen legs and catches flies?
   (A baseball team)

2. If a dad sent his son to college these days and paid thousands of dollars a year to put him through, how much change might he get back?
   (He might get a quarter-back)

3.   Why is a game of baseball like a cake?
     (Success depends on the batter)

4.   Where is the largest diamond in Boston found?
     (On the baseball field)

5.   Why did Babe Ruth make so much money?
     (A good batter makes good dough)

6.   Why did the golfer wear two pairs of pants?
     (In case he got a hole-in-one)

7.   What does a fat cat and a basketball have in common?
     (Both are small, round, and frequently stuffed)

8.   Why isn't the basketball team allowed to eat in the school cafeteria?
     (Because the players dribble)

9.   What does a cheerleader eat for lunch before a basketball game?
     (Cheerios)

10. What is a monster's favorite team?
     (Giants)

11. Does it take longer to run from first base to second or from second to third?
     (From second to third because there's a shortstop in the middle)

12. Why did the football coach run into the phone booth?
     (To get his quarterback)

13. On a baseball team, which player makes the best pancakes?
     (The batter)

14. Why was Cinderella kicked off the baseball team?
     (She ran away from the ball)

15. What did the basketball player do with his doughnut?
     (He dunked it)

16. "Who whipped the Philistines?"
     Student: "If they don't play the _____ *(local team)* I don't keep track of 'em."

17. Athlete: A dignified bunch of muscles unable to carry out the trash or clean a room.

18. Definition of a guy who loves to fish: A Finatic!

19. "What position does your son play on the football team?
   ("I'm not sure, but I think he's one of the drawbacks.")

20. A golfer is one who lugs 25 pounds of equipment several miles, but has his wife bring him a cup of coffee.

21. A girl learning to ski: "By the time I learned to stand up, I couldn't sit down!"

22. A tennis court is the only place in the world where love means nothing.

23. Know what happened to the javelin thrower who sat on his javelin?
   (He got the point)

24. Lack of experience: The assumption that you're going to be using the same ball after 18 holes of golf.

25. Baseball is discussed quite a bit in the Bible. Eve stole first, Adam stole second, Gideon rattled the pitchers, Goliath was put out by David, and the Prodigal Son made a home run.

STAGE IDEAS

PUPPETEER WEARS APRON,
ASSISTANTS HOLD IT UP.

TELEVISION STAGE
CUT FROM CARDBOARD BOX.

HAND PUPPET STAGE

- TACK SHEET TO POLE IN FRONT.

- PLACE PLANK BETWEEN CHAIRS TO HOLD PROPS.

- TIE LINE TO CHAIRS TO HANG PUPPETS WHEN NOT IN USE.

CARD TABLE STAGE
TURN A CARD TABLE ON ITS SIDE.

PAINT SCENE ON CHURCH WINDOW
FOR PUPPETS TO PEEP THROUGH.

DOORWAY STAGE

APPLIANCE BOX STAGE

- CUT OUT TOP AND BOTTOM.
- SLIT OPEN SIDE AND MAKE PUPPET HOLE.
- USE BAR FOR SCENES.

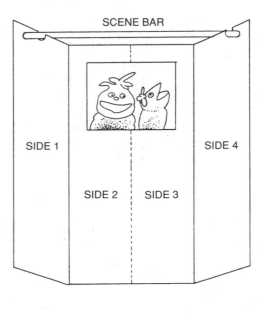

SCENE BAR

SIDE 1

SIDE 4

SIDE 2

SIDE 3

REVERSIBLE STAGE
USE WITH
MARIONETTES
OR PUPPETS.

TWO LADDERS AND A SHEET MAKE A LARGE STAGE.